CONQUERING LONELINESS

Conquering Loneliness

by
Jean and Veryl Rosenbaum

HAWTHORN BOOKS, INC.
W. Clement Stone, Publisher
NEW YORK

Contents

v

1

To Be Alone

In a recent poll of psychiatric patients more than 80 percent of those interviewed admitted that loneliness was the principal reason they sought help.

Attempted suicides run about half a million each year in the United States. Would you be surprised that the vast majority of these are triggered by loneliness?

"I can't go on—I feel so alone," read the note left by a woman who had committed suicide while still in her middle twenties. "Alone," when she lived with her parents, had a good job, and seemed to have a good future? Yes, *alone*, for investigation showed that she had no close friends and led an unsatisfactory social life; her family was not enough, not able to supply her with the outside contacts and interests she needed.

Suicide-prevention centers throughout the nation are very much aware of the part that loneliness plays in bringing people to the brink of desperation and despair. "Many times it simply helps them to be able to talk with someone," one volunteer said in explaining her work at the suicide-prevention center. "The person who feels that suicide is the only way out sometimes just needs to be able to talk things over with a sympathetic listener. Too often the person feels that he is all alone."

Workers at the Albuquerque Suicide Prevention and Crisis Center state that most of their calls are prompted by feelings of alienation and loneliness. As is typical with persons who are lonely, most of the center's calls come during the evening hours, on weekends, and on holidays. It is at those times that an individual is suddenly faced with the unalterable facts of his own loneliness and his isolation from others. Symptoms of self-pity appear, and depression sets in until the only alternative seems to be suicide.

In a statistical study done by the Los Angeles Suicide Prevention Center on youthful suicides (individuals in their teens and twenties) it was discovered that the most common factor shared by these young people was loneliness. The study involved both those who had committed suicide and those who had tried but failed.

In 1970 the national suicide rate rose 66 percent,

according to statistics compiled by the Center for Studies of Suicide Prevention at the National Institutes of Health. In 1969 the suicide rate was 7.1 per 100,000 persons, and in 1970 that figure rose to 11.8 per 100,000. Much of this increase can no doubt be attributed to the increasing pressures of modern life and technology, which tend to put barriers around people and keep them separated.

There are ways of handling your personal problems so that you are not faced with what appears to be no other choice except the final defeatist one of suicide. You can learn to recognize the strain that loneliness is placing upon your personality. You can take steps to alleviate that condition of loneliness, and that is what this book is all about: It is a handbook to help you overcome your individual loneliness problem.

Not everyone who is lonely resorts to suicide, of course, for the response to loneliness is a highly individual one. Some people overeat and become obese; others drink too much.

Walk into any meeting of Alcoholics Anonymous, and ask those assembled what caused them to start drinking.

"Loneliness drove me to it," most will reply.

Loneliness is the real culprit in drug abuse as well. A survey carried out by Drs. Lillian and Edwin S. Robbins on students in two New York City area colleges revealed that the young people who did not use drugs reported themselves as feeling much less lonely than contemporaries of theirs who used drugs.

A significant number of drug-users admit that they have turned to drugs because of feelings of extreme alienation from other members of society. Drugs, like alcohol, are the solution sought by the loner who looks for some outside force to alleviate his feelings of loneliness and depression. Like alcohol, drugs have proved to be an unsatisfactory form of relief, for although temporary help may be provided, the real problem behind the loneliness is still there when the drug-user or the drinker comes back to reality.

Moreover, loneliness is responsible for a large percentage of supposedly physical problems encountered in the average doctor's office every day. The man or woman who does not take to drugs or drink because of loneliness may instead take refuge in various psychosomatic illnesses.

Accidents and illnesses can become a way of life for the lonely person. Disability is a way to buy some attention from others. As with the more obvious responses to loneliness—alcohol, drugs, overeating, and depression—illness does not solve the basic questions of "Why am I lonely?" and "How can I get over being lonely?"

Social workers, doctors, clergymen, and trained counselors are faced daily with the problems and demands of the lonely people with whom they come in contact. There are additional thousands who never seek the help they need. They stumble along blindly, hoping that somehow they will discover ways to cope with their personal loneliness.

Unfortunately, lonely people often fail to realize how widespread this whole problem is and that they are not exceptions, nor are they even unusual. It is true that when you are lonely, you think (or at least it appears to *you*) that everyone else in the world is happy and well adjusted. "They" have friends; you don't. "They" are popular; you aren't. "They" lead such interesting lives while your life is dull and drab. If you are one of the lonely ones, you should remember not only that you can get over it, but that you are one of many sharing this common "disease."

Billy Graham said he is often asked, "What is the problem that plagues more people these days than any other?" His answer: "Loneliness."

One of America's stronger social characteristics is its attitude toward loneliness. From early infancy on, a person is trained to be a part of the group—any group—just so long as he is not found alone. So many times people will comment, "He's a strange one—spending most of his time alone."

What has caused this widespread—almost national—attitude toward being alone? Why is aloneness negative, and why is "being part of the group" considered to be a positive act? Perhaps much of the emphasis on group interaction can be traced to the early history of this country. People had to work together and stay together in order to survive. Although this was a hospitable country in many ways, it was also, particularly as the country spread westward, a hostile environment which made group action important for survival.

In pioneer and frontier days the loner was the exception. Frequently he was the bad man, the villain, or the outlaw, although even outlaws tended to band together and operate as a group. Life was simply too perilous for any except the most hardy to survive when faced with hostile and aggressive Indians, an environment that exacted a heavy toll from those who used it for subsistence, and an unknown and largely unmapped country.

These natural conditions therefore imposed a necessity upon the individual for group action and cooperation. At the same time the rigors of new-country living also brought about a great deal of emphasis on individual decisions and self-reliance. As a result of this double-pronged demand upon people, a dichotomous and confused national philosophy has emerged. Both group culture and individualism are stressed and prized, yet they are basically in opposition to each other. Personal loneliness is one result of this dichotomy.

From survival to sociability is a long step, but it happened, and when the country became safe, group culture was already firmly established. The United States has become known as the home of "togetherness," whether it is in the family circle, the ethnic group, the church denomination, or the professional organization.

This attitude is seen in the popular slogans "The family that prays together stays together," "The family that plays together stays together," and so on.

Since this is the great American ideal, it is not surprising that children are encouraged from infancy to think in terms of group life and behavior. As children progress through adolescence toward adulthood, every effort is made to keep them oriented toward the group. Social activities, clubs, and group sports are made mandatory for most youngsters.

Even in the current rebellion against the establishment and all it has come to mean in culture and standards, there is the tendency on the part of the rebels to band together and continue to operate within the framework of the group-living pattern. Thus, we have a prevalence of communes and other cooperative ventures among the hippies and others who hold antiestablishment philosophies.

One reason why hippies form groups is to get away from the loneliness they feel as persons outside the established social order. Being with others who share their views and life-style helps to make them feel less lonely. Also, like the early pioneers, they feel that their chances of survival in a hostile world are better if they stick together.

It has become a paradox that in such hippie communes there have developed both extreme group interdependence and an emphasis on individual meditation. But this current attitude is only a continuation of that earlier dichotomy between individualism and group cooperation, whether in a family, a wagon train of emigrants, or a band of explorers, trappers, or outlaws.

There has never been a clear enough understanding of the difference between aloneness and solitude. Solitude is creative and positive in both its action and its effect. Instead we hear persons say, "Isn't it a shame? George is sitting up in the apple tree reading books when he should be out playing with other children!"

Maybe George enjoys taking trips in his imagination and is enriched by reading adventure stories! When he is satisfied with that, he will probably seek company. He should not be forced to play with others if he craves solitude. Actually, sitting up in a treetop reading a book would seem to be a more fruitful way of spending his time than crouched hypnotized by the boob tube in the company of three or four other children, each of whom in his own passive, lethargic way is having a machine manufacture his fantasies for him.

Since children take their cues from parents and other adults in their circle, they can be made to feel that being alone is strange, perhaps even bad. It is not unusual to find that a child whose natural inclinations lead him to play alone in an imaginative way grows in a short time to distrust this natural instinct because his parents have convinced him that he should not spend time alone. The parents' fear that playing alone will mark their child as strange is communicated to the child until he, too, feels that life is good and normal only when he is acting in concert with other children or adults. Therefore, unless he is fortunate enough to be always surrounded by people when he becomes an adult, he may easily become despondent when left to his own devices. At best, he will be uneasy until he can once again establish some form of contact with at least one other person. At worst, he may become emotionally disturbed if circumstances force him to live or work alone.

This is what happened to Greg. He had been pushed into all kinds of group activities and social events as a child and adolescent. From home he went to a small school where he was surrounded by fellow students. Greg enjoyed college life and in particular life in the fraternity. From college he went to military service, where again he was surrounded by many people and had planned activities. He appeared to be a well-adjusted adult, but after leaving the army and going to work, Greg became emotionally disturbed. Why? Nothing in Greg's life and training had prepared him to live alone or to be on his own. When he went to a strange city and worked for a large business firm, Greg was unable to bear his new state of loneliness. He did not know what to do with his spare time. He did not know how to plan his own activities. He found that he was living with a stranger —himself. He was miserable until he had been in the city long enough to establish some group contacts. Significantly, his first contact was through a group-therapy meeting, and this in turn led to other contacts. Two years after coming to the city Greg was again a happy, well-adjusted person in terms of his own personality. He still had the problem of being alone and not liking it, but he had coped with it by becoming part of several closely knit groups. To further insure that he would not be left alone, Greg was engaged to be married.

It was his early conditioning that had made Greg the kind of adult he was, and his parents were to blame for his inability to face being alone. Unfortunately it has been observed that persons like Greg tend to hand down to their children the same attitudes toward aloneness that they received from their parents. It becomes a never-ending cycle of personality dependence.

There is nothing strange about enjoying solitude. It is rather an example of a person's solid sense of self. We are not referring to people who seek to avoid others because it is their wish to withdraw from life. That kind of person is one who is regarded clinically as a "depressed" individual, someone who has suffered loneliness for so long a time that the condition has become for him a patterned norm.

There is a significant difference between someone who prizes his solitude and achieves enjoyment from being by himself and the person who apparently has no other choice, his emotional energy being consumed by his depression. The depressed person says, "I don't care about anything."

How, one might ask, does a person attain the emotional security that enables him to deny his training? How, contrary to the edicts of a society that commands him to busy himself in the company of others, does he learn to accept, even to treasure, the pleasure of his own company?

This sense of self-reliance and self-esteem should begin in early childhood, for in order to realize the value of time spent alone and to appreciate solitude, one must have a large fund of inner resources. This means having a feeling of independence from others —being able to take care of oneself and appreciate oneself without needing someone else to validate one's existence.

"I never found the companion that was so companionable as solitude. We are for the most part more lonely when we go abroad among men than when we stay in our chambers. A man thinking or working is always alone, let him be where he will." Those words were written by Henry David Thoreau, the classic example of the man who not only preferred to be alone but knew how to make the most of his solitude. A naturalist, writer, and philosopher, Thoreau believed that the true nature of man could not be revealed through busyness and group activities. He insisted that for each man there was a unique life-style which he could discover for himself only through meaningful solitude. Thoreau was, of course, not the first or last person to proclaim these values, but he has become one of the best known, because, unlike many others, he put his ideas into practice in his own life. He also wrote extensively about his life and his philosophy, and his influence has extended far beyond the shores of his beloved Walden Pond, where he carried out his experiment in solitary living.

Most of us have the same potential for creative solitude that Thoreau had, but too often we have allowed ourselves to be conditioned by society to think that aloneness means misery means loneliness.

If a child is loved as a baby—held, rocked, fed, and cuddled—his feelings of worth begin to grow. The world is not such a bad place if, when one is hungry and cold, Mother is there with her loving attentions and ministrations. As the child grows in a loving atmosphere, he begins to carry a feeling of security within himself. A child thus loved and nurtured can content himself playing alone without Mother's constant presence.

One day, while making home visits connected with a maternity clinic, we visited Jessica. She had one child and was settling in with her new baby. When we arrived, the two-year-old, Bonnie, was sitting at the kitchen table playing with water paints. Jessica was in the living room nursing the baby. The scene was serene. Upon our entrance Bonnie came in to say hello, stayed a few minutes, and returned to her art-work. It was obvious that neither the new baby nor the visitation of strangers threatened her feelings of self-esteem. She had things to do!

When she completed a picture, she brought it in to show to us, was praised and kissed, and then skipped off to find her doll.

If Bonnie had not felt loved, she would have been angry at her mother, jealous of the new baby, and irritated by the intruders. She would have cried and whined, insisting on disrupting our conversation. There would have been no inner resources to help her through the experience of accepting a new child in the family. But she already knew how to enjoy being alone, even before the arrival of the new baby. Her internal sense of security will remain with her all her life, because once love is given in childhood, it becomes emotional glue in stabilizing the whole personality.

If you know any creative people, you will notice that it is imperative for them to be alone much of the time in order for them to express their talents. If you question them as to how they feel about work-ing alone, they will tell you of the great joy they ex-perience in the solitary creative process. Do you think Michelangelo would have been able to complete his commissioned decoration of the Sistine Chapel if he had needed to be in company with other people all the time? Could Jesus Christ have formulated the mes-sage of hope set forth in his Sermon on the Mount if he had been constantly surrounded by crowds of his followers? We know he retired to the mountain fastnesses for solitary prayer and meditation. Is it conceivable that Abraham Lincoln scribbled off the text of the Gettysburg Address while in the midst of a committee meeting? All the great works of art, music, literature, and philosophy were given to us by people having a mastery of the art of creative solitude.

You may say, "What about the majority of us who are tone-deaf, tongue-tied, and can't draw a straight line? What do we have to gain by being alone?"

For one thing you can get a firm grasp of your own mental health. You should contrive to spend some part of every day all by yourself. You will grow spiritually and emotionally if a part of each day is spent in solitary meditation and contemplation. These disciplines are like water to a budding flower. They encourage insight into your behavior and an understanding and acceptance of life's mystery. Even though being alone runs contrary to the usual tenets of our overly social society, psychoanalysts are convinced that this dimension lacking in American life—the ability to lend oneself to solitary thought and reflection—is one of the major causes of emotional illness in our culture.

For example, there is an order of nuns, the Carmelite Sisters, who have devoted their lives to meditation and prayer for the whole world. These dedicated women are deeply committed to the art of meditation and expend their love energies for the good of us all. Even though we adhere to no formal orthodox religion, as psychoanalysts we have had the opportunity of studying this Carmelite sisterhood in great depth. Most people, Catholic or non-Catholic, would suppose persons thus constrained to be weird, withdrawn, antisocial, and most of all, lonely. Quite the opposite is true. As a group as well as individually these nuns are joyful, loving individuals, for they have trained themselves in the art of self-sustaining meditation and the solitary exaltation of the human spirit.

Each of us needs a segment of each day set aside for contemplative exercise. We are constantly deluged by too many people, too much noise, too many smells, and even our eyes have to take in an overabundance of sights. These daily intrusions on the senses are called ego impingements. In other words, it takes such a considerable amount of emotional energy to ward off this constant barrage that one begins to feel drained by the pressures of the world.

It is necessary to turn away now and again to seek a quiet place within yourself to regain your strength. Children will eventually understand the pleasure of being alone when they observe their parents' own rejuvenation after a solitary respite.

Even when there are others around, it is possible to find a place of solitude. The Japanese people with all their vastly overcrowded living accommodations have, by necessity, created an invisible shield of privacy which is respected by all. If they can do this in the midst of extreme overpopulation, we, who have more than any nation in terms of room, can find a spot for solitude.

What does one do when meditating? For the moment close your eyes and shut off your ears to all intrusive stimuli. Then, to begin with, examine the thought, "To whom have I shown love today? If I have been unable to share my goodness with anyone, what can I do to make this sharing possible?"

Try it: It will begin to enhance your life.

CHAPTER

2

Nobody Loves Me

What is loneliness, anyway? The dictionary defines it as a state characterized by a depressing feeling of being alone. A woman patient once defined it as "complete despair." Another patient called it "an emotional feeling of loss which makes you feel physically ill." Thomas Wolfe in his "The Anatomy of Loneliness," which appeared in the October, 1941, issue of *American Mercury*, wrote: "The whole conviction of my life now rests upon the belief that loneliness, far from being a rare and curious phenomenon, peculiar to myself and to a few other solitary men, is the central and inevitable fact of human existence."

Yet knowing that loneliness is so universal is a rather minor consolation during periods of loneliness. The feeling of loneliness becomes so strong, so intense, that nothing else matters.

Loneliness goes through two stages or levels. First of all, it is a state of mind that disturbs the hope of happiness to come. The lonely person says, "No one cares for me." If there are no active steps taken to conquer what we are calling loneliness, the next level of unhappiness is the feeling of despair. A certain knowledge invades the heart that there is no way out of loneliness and that nothing good will ever happen in life. There is a pervasive impression that something terrible is in store for the future. The despairing person feels totally helpless and hopeless in the face of his certain fate, that of being lonely all his life. The despairing person bends under this pervasive threat and says, "No one will *ever* care for me." Again, loneliness and despair are passive states of mind that can be overcome only by active means.

If these feelings of desperation are allowed to run unchecked, they can become the psychiatric illness that is called depression. Although most lonely people are depressed, there are some differences between depression and loneliness.

Depression is real withdrawal from life. The lonely person is still trying to participate in life, even though he may be on the outer periphery of activities.

The lonely individual wallows in his misery like an animal in mire. He is very much aware of it; it surrounds him, and he becomes part of it. The depressed person may not be as conscious of his feelings of despair, because he tends to escape into a limbo of his own creation that dulls his capacity for experiencing pain.

Being lonesome does not mean being unaware. The lonely individual is often only too much aware of other people and what they are doing—always in contrast to his own miserable state of aloneness and isolation. But in depression there is a withdrawal from one's own self as well as from others. There is an unconscious rejection of the outside world. A dull darkness overtakes the soul of the depressed person, and in reality he becomes truly alone.

By way of example let us look at two cases: A. is suffering from loneliness, and B. is suffering from depression. Both individuals are unhappy and in pain from their emotional states. This unhappiness is magnified on the weekend, when all normal routines are suspended and they are faced with themselves and their particular problems. A., although lonely, maintains a kind of contact with the world at large. He takes a walk, visits the zoo, goes to a restaurant, shops, attends church, watches television, and reads the newspapers, a few magazines, and a book. Now, while he is doing these things, A. is still conscious of his feeling of loneliness. He wishes that he were not alone. At times he has fantasies in which he sees himself surrounded with others who are his friends or with one person who is attached to him in some familial, friendly, or romantic way. A. sees other people enjoying themselves during the weekend, and he is envious when he sees a couple, a family, or a group. He yearns to be a part of others' lives, an object of concern and interest.

After his weekend alone, A. cannot honestly say he has enjoyed it, but he gets up and goes to work on Monday. He carries his loneliness with him like a scar. It mars his life and his enjoyment of life, but he is still able to work and to perform other tasks. He still has some measure of self-esteem. He washes himself, dresses properly, and eats.

The same weekend may find B., the depressed person, behaving in a very nonsocial way. B., also lonely, no longer has an interest in the world around him, and his awareness of other things, people, and events has almost completely vanished. On the weekend B. may go home and sit in a kind of emotional stupor. He is not interested in eating. He does not bother to turn on the television. Books and magazines go unread and mail unanswered. Although there may be activities that B. would like to participate in during his free hours, he is unable to make the effort to go out and do things. All of his energy is channeled into a morass of despair.

On Monday B. may not be able to report for work, or if he does, his work may be inefficient, because he cannot perform effectively as a thinking person. In time, if his depression becomes severe enough, he will cease to take any interest in his personal appearance or cleanliness. In his own eyes he becomes a nonperson, not worthy of any care or consideration.

If A. in his loneliness is like a faulty machine which is operable but not up to standard, B. is a broken machine, totally incapable of any useful function.

But are all depressions so dramatically devastating? No, some periods of depression are inevitable in the average person's travel through life. No one is going to be happy about a lost job, the death of a friend, a disaster in the family. We all feel sad when seemingly insurmountable problems arise, but this is only natural. These are what psychiatrists label situational reactions. They are a part of life. Rather, we are talking about people, like B., who feel nothing else but their depression, regardless of what is happening around them. There are more of such people every day, sprinkled generously through all strata of American society.

Why is depressive loneliness so widespread in this country? There are a number of reasons, and one, of course, is the orientation toward group culture which we discussed in Chapter 1. Another reason is the almost overwhelming size of this country. The individual cannot help feeling dwarfed by the magnitude of the geography; this only contributes to his feeling of loneliness. In the back of every lonely person's mind there is the knowledge that he could easily slip away and be lost in the vastness of the country. I am not talking about being lost in the geographic sense, although that, too, is possible, but lost in an emotional sense. The lonely person can move to a new locale, and so large is this country that his former associates will no longer have any contact with him or even know of him.

The overcrowded conditions of our urban areas also contribute to the depression felt by lonely people. In fact, overpopulation becomes a rapid breeder of depression. Psychologically and emotionally the person who is lonely has a deeper sense of depression and alienation when he is surrounded by large numbers of people, none of whom seem interested in him. Many lonely people to whom I have talked stressed the fact that it was the impersonality of urban life that upset them the most.

A typical case is that of Betty G. Like many bright young women, she came to a large city following her college graduation. Getting a job was no problem, but making friends was, and Betty soon found herself feeling lonely and depressed. She lived alone in a small apartment and worked in a large and busy office where most of the other people were married and had already well-established social lives and friendships. Shy by nature, Betty found it more and more difficult to cope with her life. She began to hate her job and her apartment. At the same time her depressed loneliness drove her in rather than out, and she made no attempt to meet other people.

When I saw Betty, she was thin, withdrawn, and prone to crying spells. She was also depressed because she felt that she had failed herself by not being able to adjust to urban life. Like many other people, Betty had to learn that there are special ways of living in the big city that can help the person alone to survive in an emotional sense. Once she had learned to put aside her feelings of failure and self-pity, Betty was able to look for areas in which she could participate in activities with others. She eventually became involved in two groups—a church-related study group and a volunteer organization that worked with the physically handicapped. Through her participation in these groups Betty not only had less time to brood about her loneliness but was no longer actually alone. She began to make friends with others and in time met another girl with whom she later shared an apartment.

Unfortunately, many such stories do not end as happily as Betty's did, for too often the lonely individual refuses to seek help or make any effort to change his condition. It becomes easier to sit down and blame the world for personal loneliness than to try to break out of the depression. It becomes easier to take several drinks, to resort to drugs, or to use some other emotional crutch than to expend energy in changing life habits.

One woman who successfully recovered from depressive loneliness said, "One day I decided that if people weren't going to seek me out—and it was obvious that they weren't or I wouldn't have been so lonely—I would have to seek *them* out." For this woman it meant making the effort to find other people with whom she could share mutual interests. She started a lunch-hour drama-discussion group among fellow employees. This later became a large club, drawing members from all over the city, with regular weekly meetings at night and attendance at various city theatrical affairs.

The lonely individual, particularly if he is living in a big city, has to be able to accept the fact that he himself will have to find the solution to his own loneliness problem. He has to accept responsibility for himself.

A fourth factor that contributes to the high rate of depressive loneliness in this country is the climate of busyness and drive which produces a form of national overactivity. To the lonely individual there seems to be no time for him and his problems. Here again, the only answer is for the lonely individual to get involved with others in various activities. The more he stays by himself, the lonelier and the more depressed he will become. Being lonely in a busy world is like being in a foreign country where everyone else is speaking a strange language. You can, however, learn a foreign language so that you can communicate with people, and you can also learn the art of personal involvement.

Although no large-scale survey has been made, individual doctors, clergymen, counselors, and social workers all report that loneliness is the number-one problem with which they must deal in their contacts with people. And although no formal statistics exist, it has been estimated by the experts in these fields of counseling that loneliness now affects at least 75 percent of the population. Chronic loneliness as a part of the American scene has increased dramatically since the Korean War and is one further reflection of these unsettled times.

Loneliness, then, although it is a negative condition, is rampant. It is an emotional disease that has reached epidemic proportions. Because most lonely people remain in isolation or try to conceal their feelings, the high number of those affected by this disease is not always recognized. A friend of mine once said that if all lonely people suddenly woke up to find the color of their skin changed to the same blue as their mood, the world as a whole would be shocked at the vast number of "blue," or lonely, people. But because loneliness is negative, it can best be defeated by the use of positive weapons.

Now that we have explored various aspects of aloneness and the private self, let us examine the pride of fulfillment that one can realistically expect through relationships with others.

One of the goals of psychoanalysis is to help patients to be able to love to the best of their ability. To love another person means to have the capacity of sharing yourself with him. There is no such thing as one-sided love, because love, if it is mature, has a mutual quality of giving and receiving.

Many lonely people say, "I have no one who loves me" or "If only someone cared about me." Do you detect a one-sided note of childish demand in these statements? Why do they not say, "I wish I cared about or loved someone" or "I wish I had someone to share my love with"? This is certainly a more mature and outgoing attitude than sulkily complaining that no one cares.

Why do so many people seem unable to develop mature relationships with other people? It is usually because they have not developed a mature relationship with themselves first. Frequently they don't keep themselves mentally alert. They often dislike themselves but cover up that feeling by transferring it to a dislike of their environment. They won't accept any blame for their lonely situation. Almost universally, they expect other people to solve their problems for them. And although they don't find themselves very interesting, they expect other people to be interested in them and their lives. The truth is that if you are still living with the emotional attitudes and demands of a child, you cannot expect to have a satisfactory relationship with another adult. The lonely person is frequently the emotionally spoiled person who wants everything but does not know how to give anything in return.

It is a fact of life that the only time one is loved without having to return it is during infancy. Infants are normally selfish, self-centered, and totally demanding. The tyrannical demands of the infant's need to be fed and cared for are met by the mother's unstinting love and service, which asks no return. At no other state in a person's life is love given without being earned.

As an adult you cannot expect to continue to receive that same kind of love. Adult love implies responsibility. Love is the property only of the deserving. When you wish for the love of some vague "someone," interrupt your daydreaming for a moment and ask yourself candidly what qualities you would wish this someone to possess.

Is it a person who will listen to your woes and share your self-pity? A lover who will see beyond your shortcomings and accept the "real you" completely and unconditionally, without your having to lift a hand to earn that love and approbation? How much is expected of this someone, and in what particulars do you wish to be served? Are you looking for someone with whom you can share loneliness rather than adult life and mature love?

These are important questions for you to answer, for only you can know the real extent of your loneliness problem and the attitudes you have developed toward it and toward others in relation to your loneliness. One way in which you are going to be able to help yourself is to ask some relevant questions. Asking the questions is, of course, only one step—the first step. The second step is listening to your own answers. Those answers are going to give you the necessary clues about your loneliness—clues you need in order to help solve your problem.

Be honest with your answers. Nothing is gained by investing your patterns of yearning with nobler motives than do, in fact, exist. If your answers seem filled with a strong need to be accepted and cared for, you will meet with certain disappointment. That loving, all-giving, one-sided relationship—or the personification of it in some dreamed-of "someone"— exists only in fantasy. In your imaginings of the lover ideal you have defined a mother or father image and a relationship that is nothing more than a nostalgic memory from childhood.

While you are hiding in your room wearing a mask of indifference, does this idyllic someone appear in a guise of adulation and say, "Ah, at last I have found you, and I will take care of all your needs. Just stand there and be marvelous *you!*"? The absurdity of such a fantasy is self-evident, yet it is common among people who don't want to give love and wish to retreat instead behind a futile dream of being discovered by "someone who cares."

Now, let's reverse the roles. Place yourself in the position of this "someone." Would you be willing to be so giving and accepting of another person while receiving no emotional feedback? Well, hardly! Unless there is something seriously wrong with you. Only a pathological martyr who fears meaningful involvement chooses to give and give while receiving nothing in return. There could certainly be no real love or friendship in the mature sense. The receiver would be nothing more than a dependent child who is in your power. Would an emotionally healthy person desire such a relationship? This is *love*?

As an adult you should expect to give and receive love in a meaningful relationship. The kind of relationship that you daydream about, however, may indicate your level of emotional inscurity. You would feel ridiculous if you went around sucking your thumb because you felt emotionally upset, yet when you project this negative image of love and companionship, it is the same thing. You show that you are seeking a dependency relationship with another person because you feel so inadequate. What you are looking for is not a lover, not a friend, but a keeper!

You must be realistic about what you expect from relationships with other people. What have *you* to offer that will enhance someone else's joy of life?

If you are so consumed with self-pity that you answer "nothing," then you are not willing to fight your loneliness. Everyone has something to share with someone. If you have eyes, you can share with the blind. If you have time, you can share it with the sick, who feel that your moments spent with them are more precious than all the flower arrangements in the world. If you have a little love to give, the world needs you now!

If you have considered this concept, however, and still feel that you are lonely, then much of your loneliness problem can be traced to your self-image. Self-image is the way in which you look at yourself. It usually has no resemblance to the way in which other people see you, although in some cases the self-image you have is projected so that it can influence other people's thinking about you as a personality. One of the things you are trying to do in asking and answering these questions about yourself is to determine what kind of a self-image you have. The lonely person is inclined to have a poor or faulty self-image.

If you have problems with your self-image, think of it as you would a faulty television picture. Your self-image may be distorted, blurred, or lacking in sharp detail. And just as you would take steps to correct a faulty picture on the television screen, you can take steps to correct your poor self-image. Your first objective should be to try to determine through the process of self-exploration the exact conformation of your self-image and why you have the picture of yourself that you have. Again, like the questions and answers, this requires honesty on your part, an honesty that may be painful.

In your self-exploration try to see yourself with some objectivity. What do you do in thought and action to keep yourself feeling rejected and lonely? Be honest. If someone happens to remark, "There are some people who never bathe" or "There are some people who have bad breath," do you automatically *know* they are referring to you? With all the people there are in the world, what kind of egotism causes you to suppose you are the one being talked about?

If you are this self-centered, you deserve to collect insults!

There is no better way to keep yourself feeling hurt and rejected than to attach to yourself any vague, thoughtless scrap of criticism that you can use in the service of your agony. This slight-gathering is encouraged by your punitive superego which says, "See, they *are* talking about you! You failed to take a bath today, and everybody knows. Shame on you! No wonder you are without friends. Dirty, dirty!"

It's doubtful that you are offending anyone for having missed your bath. The commercial soap and cosmetic industries capitalize on programs of intimidation of this kind. They would have you believe yourself a social pariah if you neglect to use their product. Normal body odor is neither so common nor so offensive as the advertisements maintain.

While you are taking this look at your self-image and your attitude toward yourself, you should also ask why you have such a low opinion of yourself. Does this self-deprecation come from some childhood experience? Is it from some traumatic incident which left you with a lasting impression of your own unworthiness? One adolescent discovered that he considered himself to be, in his own words, "of no account" because of a shoplifting incident when he was a youngster. Not only had he been severely punished by his parents but they had remarked about him in front of other family members that they con-

sidered him to be "dishonest and no good." What this
had done to his self-image was to give him a mental
picture of himself that echoed their words. It kept
him from succeeding in his relationships with other
people. "I thought nobody could ever like me because
I was such a bad person," he explained.

Your self-image may be reflecting disappointment
with your life and situation. One man who was extremely lonely admitted that he deliberately avoided
people because he felt sensitive about his lack of
education. In his own eyes he was a failure because
he had not finished school. "And nobody likes a
failure!" he insisted. His problem, as with thousands
of other people who have faulty self-images, was his
inability to accept and live with himself realistically.
The problem with disliking or feeling ashamed of
yourself is that you can't ever really get away from
your own personality; like the snail's shell, it is always
with you as long as you live.

Your self-critical eye is constantly seeking situations to prove to you how unworthy you are, to keep
you enslaved in loneliness. Do you honestly believe
that the people you associate with are as preoccupied
with your faults as you are? They have their own to
deal with and are usually inclined to overlook your
shortcomings if you do the same for them. But maybe
what you are looking for is human perfection. Are
you as critical of your acquaintances as you are of
yourself? If this is the case, then you *are* in trouble!
The impractical idealist in search of human perfec-

tion is bound to be a loser. No such animal exists. The best you can do is to blind yourself to all the annoying imperfections you find in your acquaintances and start looking for the good traits they are sure to possess. Just as no one is wholly perfect, there is no one totally lacking in redeeming good qualities. Apply this rule to yourself, and begin a program of improvement of the good points you are sure to recognize once you put aside your negative evaluation of yourself.

Familiarity with another person, such as someone you live with or work closely with day after day, causes peculiarities of personal appearance gradually to become unnoticeable. What you tend to notice more is the manner of treatment displayed toward you—whether cross and impatient, pleasant and caring, and the like. If you are always worried about your looks (nose too long, hair stringy and discolored, ears too big, or whatever irregularities of feature or physical makeup keep you feeling self-consciously inferior), just remember that the image you have of your body is pretty well going to coincide with the way you picture yourself, and this will be reflected in your personality. One's physical appearance is important. Nothing so much bolsters self-esteem as the certainty that you are looking your best. But it isn't the total picture.

If you are too fat and use this as a rationalization for your despair, then diet. This will not by itself alleviate your loneliness, but it will give you a needed

boost to your self-esteem and the physical prepared-
ness to move on. Make yourself as attractive as you
can with such physical assets as you possess, then
forget about it. As one noted counselor whose syndi-
cated column is read by millions put it, "To marry a
person because he or she is beautiful or handsome is
the same as a starving man purchasing a bowl of
plastic fruit."

In your sessions of self-exploration see if you can
recall where you acquired the picture of yourself as
an ugly duckling. Did one of your parents compare
your appearance unfavorably with that of one of
your siblings, a cousin, or a neighbor child? Did a
brother or sister tell you you were the ugliest kid
they ever saw? Think back to see what reason may
have been behind such a crushing statement. Perhaps jealousy because you could run faster or make
better grades in school. All that was so long ago. Now
that you know the answer, can't you just laugh it
off? And the next time you are looking your best
and ready to venture forth with self-confidence and
that put-down voice inside whispers, "How can you
expect to have friends with that disaster of a face—
stay home with your head in a sack and do the world
a favor," it's your cue to say, "Go to hell!"

Who are you? What do you really want to give to
other people? Or to receive from them? If you excuse your noninvolvement with the complaint that no
one would really like you even if you were able to
reach out to them, then what you really mean is that

you don't like yourself. Why not? If there are qualities in your personality that you find unlovable, characteristics you yourself deplore, then of course you cannot expect others to love you for them either. But be honest with yourself. No one is without faults. What do you find about yourself that is so unpleasant that it "turns people off"? Are your imperfections all *that* special?

Rebecca J. complained that no one ever approached her to begin a conversation at the many business-connected cocktail parties she attended. She was resentful because she dressed well and knew she was attractive, and yet she could see men talking with women she felt to be quite homely.

To try to get to the root of the problem, we asked her to pretend she was at a party and to look and feel as she would do if she were there. Without her being aware of it, her face took on an expression of superior disdain—a look that would make anyone hesitate to approach her. She was her own enemy. This look was a defense she automatically assumed to cover up her real need of other people. The look said, "I dare you to try to talk to me! I don't need anyone." Of course, people would much rather get to know someone who looks pleasant and inviting; life is too short to bother with someone who looks threatening.

Rebecca's problem, obviously, was a basic fear of being rejected by people. In order to avoid this potential rejection by exposing her feelings of loneliness, she appeared disdainful of them (the sour-grape syn-drome), thus setting up a self-perpetuating cycle of loneliness. When she finally decided to take a risk in life and present herself as an interested warm person, she soon was making friends. Rather than wait for others to approach her, she herself started the conversations and found herself putting others at ease. Newly armed with a smile and a willingness to listen to others, she was able to escape from her self-built cage.

You can extricate yourself, too. The key is to be honest with yourself and to have a genuine desire to change those qualities in your personality that you know are unappealing. This is not so very difficult. Think of it as a housecleaning of personality litter to make room for better furnishings, so that you may entertain others and enjoy love and friendship.

Beverly knew she was very lonesome for friends. She could not understand why people avoided her. She wasn't in the least shy and always started the conversational ball rolling. She had many interests and hobbies and an exciting job and was well read and knowledgeable about current events. We, too, were puzzled to understand the reason for her lack of friends.

Then one evening we saw her at a lecture on en-vironment and witnessed her behavior during the social and discussion period. She was aware and interested in ecology and spoke well in voicing her opinions. The trouble was that she usurped the conversation, allowing no one else to express his ideas on the subject. Her sentences flew into each other with such rapidity that it was impossible to share or take part in the discussion. She was in love with her own mind and voice. Of course, people resented being talked *at*. Gradually the circle around her drifted away, and she was left alone again.

It is understandable that when a person lives alone, he may want to talk a great deal when he finds himself with company. But we must share conversation in order to earn the right of dialogue, respect, and the blossoming of friendship. Do people's eyes seem to glaze over with boredom as you expound your opinions? Do you really listen to their views, or do you just hear them out, waiting for an opening that will give you the floor again so you can expound your own philosophy?

Conversation is a sharing of ideas through verbal exchange, not an opportunity to show off your intellect. Can you listen? Do you invite an exchange of opinions? Are you really interested in anyone other than yourself? Be honest and grow! The choice is a personal, vital one. You can resolve your infantile longing for an unrealistic relationship. You can gain a place in the adult world of mutual giving and receiving, a world in which aloneness is respected but loneliness is recognized as a disease of the past.

3

Temporary Loneliness

Perhaps you have not suffered any great amount of loneliness in the past, and now you suddenly find yourself confronted by a void of loneliness because of a critical change in your life. You are probably alarmed by the intensity and suddenness with which an attack of loneliness can assail you, and you fear that this feeling will persist.

This loneliness may be so overpowering that you become physically ill. As a result of it, you may discover unexpected symptoms of physical distress, such as sleeplessness, indigestion, loss of appetite, or extreme fatigue. These physical feelings plus your emotional state will cause depression.

This is the temporary kind of loneliness which we call situational. It usually comes from some change in your environment. It is accompanied by feelings of emptiness and some bewilderment. Patients going through this state frequently complain of not being able to make decisions. They are in a position similar to a leaf being whirled downstream. They know only that their lives have been suddenly changed in some way by some event, and they feel temporarily helpless. Fortunately, by definition, people suffer for only a limited period from situational loneliness, for either the condition that has caused it ceases, or they learn to cope with the changes in their lives.

In addition to depression, emotional fatigue, and confusion, situational loneliness can produce temporary changes in an individual's personality. These changes, which are usually negative, include apathy, hostility, irritation, and emotional instability. An individual feels a loss of self-identity and has difficulty in communicating with others. As a result of these feelings, the situationally lonely person may do or say things not in keeping with his usual standards of conduct. He may turn to alcohol, drugs, food, or sexual activity in an attempt to forget his "new" condition of loneliness. It is also not unusual for such an individual to relapse into periods of sullenness or to become withdrawn and exhibit classic signs of suspiciousness toward others.

The intense feelings experienced during periods of temporary loneliness are the same as those of a person who has lived in loneliness for a long time, but they are caused by a reaction to some external situation rather than being an internal pattern of life.

What kinds of things cause situational loneliness? As I have already indicated, any change will do it, but particularly a sudden change. However, even anticipated changes may prove to be disastrous, especially if there are strong emotional connections associated with those changes. For example, parents know that their children will grow up and leave home, yet too often when this does occur, parents find themselves unable to cope with this change in family life.

Situational changes in the family can include marriages, divorces, deaths, illnesses, and any absences of loved ones for other reasons. Any change of location from neighborhood, city, or country can cause temporary loneliness; so can a change in job, even within the same company. Many people experience situational loneliness for the first time in their lives when they retire.

These are feelings that are, or will be, experienced by all of us sometime during our lives. Every human being meets with some situation that brings on an attack of loneliness which ordinarily is only temporary. Changes of condition or environment are as much a part of life as birth and continuity. How you handle your temporary loneliness is a fair gauge of how emotionally stable you are.

To be emotionally stable or mature means that you can successfully handle changes or aspects of change in your life. In other words, you don't panic when the normal routines and patterns of your life are altered by outside circumstances. You are able not only to accept these changes but to recognize that they are the inevitable by-products of life. You understand their temporary nature and are willing to accommodate yourself both physically and emotionally to the changed circumstances. This is not to say that you are not sorry, unhappy, or perhaps even uncomfortable with the temporary changes, but it does mean that you do not stop living.

Having emotional stability means that your level of self-esteem remains at a very consistent mark. You do not lose it when confronted by some change in your life. You can accept change and still have a high regard for yourself and your capabilities. This loss or diminishing self-esteem usually occurs in persons who feel so insecure in their lives that they have to blame themselves when things don't go right or go in an unexpected pattern. I have seen such a person spend hours trying to determine what he did wrong that caused such a shift in his life pattern. True, a person does do things that cause changes, but once something is done, it cannot help to indulge in acts of self-reproach and self-recrimination. This negativism drains off self-esteem and makes emotional adjustment to temporary loneliness almost impossible.

Not being able to accept change and its accompanying loneliness because of instability and immaturity means that you are acting like a child. The child does not understand why things do not always remain the same. He is not able to understand and cope with the absence of a parent, the death of a pet, a move to a new neighborhood, the loss of a playmate, or accidents and other catastrophes that result in property damage. Any one of these things can trigger tremendous and overwhelming feelings of loneliness.

Adults, however, who should be able to understand both the nature of the event and its probable duration, should be able to cope with this type of temporary loneliness. Unlike children, they should be able to withstand the emotional shock of change, because they realize the part that change plays in life. They should be mature enough to be able to take advantage of environmental or other changes in their lives without suffering from disabling attacks of loneliness.

The result when an adult can't cope with changes and reverts to a childhood emotional state is not pleasant for others or for the person directly involved. Everyone is miserable! Mona, for example, was a burden to her family, for whenever her husband went on business trips, she became a victim of temporary loneliness. She would not keep busy at her usual tasks at home but would call her family and talk for hours about how lonely and upset she was. She neglected not only her house but her personal appearance during her husband's absences. She explained her condition by saying, "I'm just not happy and alive when Harold is gone!" It is not surprising that Mona was an extremely dependent person and as a child had been very attached to her parents. "They never got a baby-sitter for me," Mona said.

"I cried so when they left me that they got so they either took me along or we all stayed home." Mona is now a grown woman, but she is still crying.

Some people become emotionally disturbed while suffering from temporary loneliness. Alice moved to a large city and began work in a large office. Accustomed to a small town, she could not adjust to the impersonality and loneliness of the city. She became childish in her responses toward other people and began to imagine that people were gossiping about her. Later, unable to establish friendships easily, she accused people in her office of malicious conduct toward her and blamed them for her isolation and loneliness.

There are many people like Mona and Alice, but there are also people in similar circumstances, like Adele, who are able to adjust to change. When Adele's husband was transferred to another city, she was unable to go with him until they sold their house and made other arrangements. Although she was lonely, Adele kept busy at her usual activities. She was mature enough to understand that the separation was necessary and temporary. She did not waste those months in tears and emotional expressions of unhappiness. She felt, in her own words, "very much alone at times," but she did not succumb to those feelings.

At some time or another almost everyone in America moves from a familiar neighborhood to a new town or city or a different part of the country. Americans are by nature a very mobile people. Perhaps it is our immigrant background that keeps America on the move, as opposed to Europeans who, in the past at least, seemed content to remain where their family roots began.

Suddenly you are in a new city and feel a chill of unfriendliness. This is because you are unfamiliar with your surroundings. Strangers who are at home with the city and comfortable in it appear to be cold and harshly scrutinizing. This is a form of "stranger anxiety"—the same feeling of fear and distrust that infants feel toward persons who are not members of their own family.

Before passing judgment, give yourself an opportunity to get your bearings. Put your house or apartment in order; then make the effort to become a member in good standing of your new neigborhood or community. Learn where your grocery store, drugstore, bank, and gas station are located, and on your first trip to each of them introduce yourself and explain that you are a newcomer. You may be surprised at how friendly people can be when they know that you are a stranger. Don't be too timid to ask questions about your area. Most persons are actually eager to talk about their city, town, or state, and you can often receive valuable and interesting information from what you might have considered unlikely sources. I have in mind a gas-station attendant whose hobby happens to be local history. He can tell more about the area in which he lives and tell it more interestingly than any other person I know. People like to share their enthusiasm and interests, so give them that opportunity.

Some cities have "welcome wagons" with friendly people whose job is to give advice on what types of programs are available in your new community. If they fail to find you, give them a call. Look in the paper for information on the local garden club or photography meeting or any community enterprise where people with similar interests meet. Become active in these community affairs. Go with the purpose of sharing your knowledge and making friends with interesting new people.

In Florida there is a radio show by the name of *Canada Calling*. The purpose of the program is to enable Canadians—themselves strangers far from home and in a new environment—to hear of new-comers who have arrived in town. They give the names and phone numbers of folks looking for card partners or shut-ins seeking company. A patient of mine found a long-lost childhood sweetheart three blocks away after listening to *Canada Calling*. They had a warm and wonderful reunion.

One of the best ways to cope with the problem of temporary loneliness in a new environment is to promptly transfer your membership in church, lodge, or service club to your new locale. You will find a ready and warm acceptance when you go to your new church or club and bring your membership from the previous one. This has an advantage for you, because you have an immediate sharing of common interests and ideas. You may attend your first service or meeting as a stranger and newcomer, but it is almost certain that you will leave it as a friend. When you do begin to take part in these kinds of activities, listen alertly for things with which you can help. You may have had some valuable experience in community projects in your last city, and the things you learned there can be helpful to your new club or church group. Don't wait to be asked to help. Offer your services when there is going to be a special project. Working with other men and women of the community will help you to feel less lonely and will speed up the process of making new friends.

Another practical way of coping with temporary loneliness after a move is to do volunteer work at the hospital, home for the aged, or other institution. Here again, you will be making new friends easily and learning more about your new community.

Becoming involved in the community in some way, whether through church, service club, or volunteer work, is one of the best ways to become thoroughly acclimated to your new environment. Once you have become involved, you tend to forget that you are new and nervous about your strange environment. It is the quickest way I know to make yourself thoroughly at home in a new place.

One woman I know makes it a practice to become involved in the local volunteer tutoring program wherever she moves. A former schoolteacher, she finds this the best way for her to adjust to new surroundings. "I'm interested in education and in young people," she explained. "The tutoring program gives me an opportunity to become a part of my new city. I've found that one of the best ways to get to know a town is by talking to the young people. Tutoring puts me in touch with people and makes me feel useful. I don't have time to be lonely."

Your temporary loneliness can be helped and overcome if you are willing to make the effort to take those first steps toward being an interested and concerned citizen of your new community.

Keep in mind that any depth of feeling for the new people you will meet will take time to grow before developing into the kind of friendship you felt for those you knew "back home" and grew up with. You cannot expect to have that comfortable feeling with a person until you have shared time, ideas, and experiences together. Do not depend on old friends' letters to sustain you. This can hold you back from making new acquaintances and from possibilities for new growth. Wherever you are, live there with the people around you now, not in your past.

You can also help yourself to cope with the temporary loneliness caused by a move if you spend some time in preparation for the change. Naturally when you move, you have to pack, notify friends and relatives, change addresses, and do what seems to be an unending list of necessary things; these are all part of your physical move, but it is also very important that you prepare yourself emotionally.

This psychological preparation, although it will not eliminate your situational loneliness after the move, will shorten the period of loneliness. Once you have learned that you are to move, start a campaign to learn all you can about your new location. Read books and magazines about that area. Become familiar with its history and geography. Write to the local chamber of commerce, and get their leaflets and a city and county map so that you can become familiar with the streets and the location of schools, churches, and other public buildings. If you have selected a place to live in advance of your move, study the map of that neighborhood so that when you get there, you can find your way around easily. Getting lost can be a bad emotional experience and can contribute to your feelings of aloneness. The transition period can also be helped if you subscribe in advance to the local newspaper. Through the paper you can become familiar with current issues, civic events, the names of stores and local people, as well as the political and economic climate of your new area.

This premove preparation does not mean that you won't have moments of loneliness and anxiety, but they will not be so intense; nor, as I have already indicated, will they last long. It isn't easy to move, but you can learn to handle it successfully without suffering personality damage because of severe loneliness problems.

Another type of temporary loneliness often comes to women whose children have all gone their separate ways—to college, marriage, or just independently setting up their own households. This should be a time of rejoicing rather than of feeling useless. After all, our job as parents is to bring children into the world and through love and example to prepare them to leave us and seek their own life-styles. If you think differently—that young adults should still depend on you for advice and support—then you should re-examine your reasons for wanting children in the first place. Was it to have someone to take care of you in your old age? Have you been living *through* your children all these years rather than *with* them? Have you given them so much of your time and attention that there is nothing left of you but motherhood personified? What about your relationship with your husband? Has your marriage been an experience of continued growth together, or have you just existed together for the sake of the children?

If your answer is Yes to most of these questions, then you will need to change your outlook through conscious effort and thus alter your attitudes. It is an emotional shock to have dependent children grow up and leave home, but it does not need to be the end of your life. You should, instead, look on it as the beginning of a new life for yourself.

Here again, the degree of adjustment depends upon the degree of emotional maturity which a person has developed in his life. Take two almost identical cases. Mrs. A. became extremely depressed and lonely when her two children left home to attend college. She no longer displayed an interest in her church or community. She lived only for the days of vacation when her children would be home on visits, and she continually complained that they chose to go away to school instead of attending a local college. Her only life had been in her children, particularly since the death of her husband, and now that they have left her, she has in a sense allowed herself to die.

Mrs. B., also a widow, has faced the same problem but with far different results for herself, her children, and her community. "I was very lonely when my children left," Mrs. B. explained, "and for a couple of months I just did nothing but think about the way the house used to be. Then one day I realized how ridiculous this attitude was and how unbecoming for an adult! I felt embarrassed for myself and for the way I was behaving toward my children. I decided that this was really a chance for me to express myself as an individual instead of just as a mother! Art had always interested me, but I never had the time while the children were growing up to do much about that interest. I signed up for art classes, and while I'll never be a great artist, it has changed my life and given me lots of new friends and absorbed all of my spare time. Yes, I still miss my children, but only at times, and we have a better relationship because I have something to share with them instead of just making emotional demands upon them and their time."

Many women are so oriented toward home and

children that they want to continue in that familiar
pattern. This can be done without sacrificing your
past devotion to your own family and children. You
need only to be willing to expand your sphere of influence and interest. If you still feel the need to take
care of children, there are numerous agencies in cities
that are pleading for help with youngsters, where your
knowledge and experience are of highest value regardless of your age or formal education. If you want
to make a career of working with children but don't
qualify by formal training for social work, then why
not go back to school and obtain these necessary
qualifications? Indeed, why not?

Just remember, though, it takes no academic degree
to read stories to crippled children in a hospital ward.
It is appropriate for needy children to be dependent
on you for attention and substitute mothering. It is
not appropriate, nor is it realistic, to want to keep
your own growing children in a stage of infantile
dependency. Let go of the past, and join the present.
Your children will love, admire, and respect you in a
new and enriching way. Then you will have two new
and rewarding kinds of relationships that defy loneliness. After all, young people should feel no guilt
about leaving home—only pride in themselves and a
credit to their parents' good child-rearing practices.
The parents ought to be able to share in this pride of
accomplishment.

Although mothers suffer more from this kind of
temporary loneliness than fathers do, it is not unusual

for a father to feel emotionally upset when his children leave home. The degree of his loneliness will often depend upon the amount of time he devotes to outside activities and his work. I have known men who were able to fill the void in their lives after their children left by doing volunteer work with underprivileged children or by helping with a local sports and recreation program.

There is so much good work to be done in this world that it is really impossible to feel useless and lonely merely because one of your major responsibilities is completed. It only frees you for accepting some others.

There is a myth in this country that goes like this: If you work a certain number of years and put in your time joylessly, then after all those gray years you have earned your retirement and the freedom to do what you want. Many men die within a year or so of retirement, and underneath the medical cause you will often discover a history of disappointment, boredom, and loneliness in retirement. In this myth there is an assumption that work is unpleasant and that all the time in the world to play is what people really want. As our son said after spending three days sick in bed, "Staying away from school seems like fun until you have to, and then it's a real drag. There isn't much to do when everyone you know is working or playing at school." So it is with those who, having retired, find the "golden years" far from idyllic.

There are many dangers inherent in such myths as

those that surround the retirement idea. The mistaken idea that "real" living must be postponed until later is one of those dangers. Another danger is in the assumption that by some form of unknown magic all sorts of skills will develop the day after retirement. Men and women who never used their minds or hands in the pursuit of some art form or sports game will expect instantaneous success after they retire. It is like the old joke of the patient whose hands were being operated on for tumors:

"Will I be able to play the piano after the operation, Doctor?" was his question.

"Of course!" replied the doctor.

"That's good, because I don't know how to play now," exclaimed the pleased patient.

We laugh at the joke, but the reality is not funny and can often have tragic implications for the disappointed retiree.

Paul R. continually talked about what he was going to do when he retired; he intended to paint pictures, but he refused to take any steps toward learning the technique of painting. He disliked his job in a large office and spent his leisure hours watching television and dreaming of the free time he would have when retired. He saw himself as a happy and successful artist. The great day came, the farewell speeches were made, the company gift presented, and then at last Paul was free from what he had always referred to as "my slavery." The days after retirement found Paul unable to settle down to his artwork, for he simply did not know where or how to begin. He had not prepared himself in any practical way for those days of "freedom." Being retired did not automatically give him the skill and judgment he needed to begin a new career. His retirement days were filled with the same unhappiness and frustration he had experienced when he was working.

We believe that people should not retire until they have made extensive plans for a new kind of work and understand fully how different life will be when they change their activities so drastically.

In St. Petersburg, Florida, a retirement community, people line the streets, sitting on benches as if waiting for the bus to their own funeral. They look forlorn, as if they had been cheated—so much unused talent, wisdom, and love going to waste!

Plan ahead; develop new interests all through life, so that when the time comes for retirement, you don't suffer the loneliness of time on your hands and no one to share it with.

A recent survey by the U.S. Department of Health, Education, and Welfare showed that in the United States there are twenty million men and women over sixty-five years of age. There are forty-two million men and women who are in the forty-five-to-sixty-five age bracket. These millions all represent real or potential cases of loneliness. Only careful planning can help these persons adjust to the changes that age and retirement bring into their lives. John B. Martin, U.S.

Commissioner on Aging, says: "These forty-two million men and women, most at the peak of their family responsibility, careers, and earning power, must begin to think seriously about the later years of life, about what they wish to do in retirement, and to plan intelligently in order to be able to fulfill their wishes."

What are you doing to keep your "golden years" from becoming tarnished? What are you doing to prepare for the time when you no longer have your work to fill up your time?

A neighbor told me that he has taken up photography as a hobby. "I'm getting ready for my retirement now," he explained. "I suddenly realized that in about five years I will no longer have an office to go to every day. I remember how my father went downhill after he retired. His work was the only thing that seemed to matter to him, and it was pathetic to see him slowly dying of boredom. I don't intend to let this happen to me!"

Another acquaintance took up weaving so that she would be able to escape the burdens of loneliness when her teaching career would be ended by retirement.

These are individual cases. What about couples who have shared the responsibilities of family and jobs and now face retirement together?

Married couples who have worked throughout their marriage on the continued growth of their love have earned the wonderful gift of time together. They find that when the time comes to retire, their enjoyment of life and of each other is enhanced rather than lessened.

If you do not have common interests and love to share with one another, it isn't too late to improve your relationship. All you need is a desire to mend past misunderstandings. Too difficult? Takes too much time? What for? Who said that life's tasks should be easy? What else do you have but time? It is the love given and received that makes the new day a present to be opened and savored for its wonder and uniqueness!

The most wretched and difficult journey through loneliness is when a loved one is lost by death. Often we hear at funerals, "Don't cry—he would not have wanted you to be sad." This is ridiculous! You *should* cry as long as you have tears to shed. The mourning process should be fully indulged. Grief is the highest tribute to love. Tears are balm to the crushed spirit. They help heal the wounds of sadness.

Those who put off their grief will pay dearly for their repressed emotions. As long as five, ten, and twenty years later these repressed emotions of unspent grief have been known to erupt in the form of a massive depression or painful psychosomatic illness known to psychiatrists as pathological mourning reaction. It is never wise to drug yourself with sedatives in order to "get through" the funeral and the long days afterward when you are grief-stricken and life feels empty and meaningless. This is the time for unassuaged mourning.

Mourning is a time-honored ritual that is more than the purging of grief. It is the psychological burying of the dead. If you do not bury the dead, you have to carry them in your life. How long do you suppose mourning should take? Six weeks? Three months? For someone dearly loved, and particularly for someone you have been near to who has lived in the same household, two years is not an overlong time for mourning, and sometimes it may normally be even a year or two longer. On the other hand, a grief prolonged beyond a reasonable period of mourning may be motivated by self-pity and self-dramatization—an unconscious pleading for continuance of attention and expressions of sympathy.

You should go through your period of mourning and then emerge, purged of grief and depression, ready once again to assume your place in the family circle and social order. Mourning should prepare you to be able to reassume your responsibilities and duties.

Parents who have lost children through death suffer a particularly numbing kind of loneliness. In Great Britain an attempt has been made to help parents through this period of mourning by the formation of the Society of Compassionate Friends. This society, which now has twenty branches, is to help parents accept the fact of the death of their children and reshape their lives. The founder, Simon Stephens, who is a minister also trained in psychiatry, says that the purpose of the society is not only to help parents over this difficult time but also to prevent the damaging results of this particular form of loneliness. Investigations of cases by Stephens had revealed that the death of a child has often also meant the end of a marriage or the neglect of the remaining children in the family.

The subject of mourning, then, is extremely complicated and calls for careful elucidation. Americans are singularly uneducated and untrained by custom on how to accept and to handle death. Other civilizations and cultures have been better able to handle funerary rites through ceremonial systems which permitted survivors to have a mourning period. For example, in ancient Rome there was a mourning period of nine days, which was followed by a banquet at the home and offerings at the tomb. The survivors in many cultures must show their mourning by wearing special clothes and refraining from customary activities, usually for a specified period of time. During this time survivors and their friends concentrate exclusively upon the subject of their grief and their own condition of being in mourning. When the time of mourning, the length of which is determined by custom or religion, is fulfilled, they all return to normal living patterns. They have had the satisfaction of having exorcised the demon of their loss through the ritual of mourning.

In America there is an ambivalent attitude toward mourning and toward death itself. In a land where planned obsolescence of all material objects is the rule, there seems to be no room for death. In a land where violence and sudden death are constant factors, there is no time for mourning. It is these contradictions that make death in this country so difficult to accept and to mourn.

Plainly, Americans must come to terms with this subject. There is a breaking down of old taboos against death, and people are expressing their desire to talk about it and about their relation to it. Recently when the magazine *Psychology Today* issued a questionnaire to readers asking for their opinions and comments on death, they were amazed to find that over thirty thousand readers responded, some with long letters. This was far in excess of the reader response to a similar earlier questionnaire on sex. In this and similar surveys people are showing that they are concerned about their own deaths, the deaths of loved ones, and in particular what attitude they should have in reference to death. There is a growing concern with the place of the survivors. Death is being studied in all of its aspects, including the ritual of mourning. In the *Psychology Today* survey 47 percent believe that funerals are important rituals for the survivors.

How should *you* approach the loneliness of mourning?

The loneliness felt in mourning is caused by an

external situation. It has a definite reason for being and is specifically related to the loss of a loved one. There is no medication, no cure, no relief, except through time and philosophic acceptance for this kind of loneliness. You must come to a realization that life cannot be the same again and accept this fact with mature resignation. You may feel guilty when you return to your own interests and begin to enjoy people again, but renewed pleasure in life is a symptom of good mental health and should be welcomed.

Some stages in life are temporarily lonely. Two of these are adolescence and old age. We will discuss the special problems of adolescence in Chapter 8.

In the case of older people, many of them feel lonely and useless because they have become inactive with the afflictions of age and are unable to pursue life as they once did. This feeling is compounded in this country by the common tacit denial of death. The elderly are shunned because they exemplify loss of youth, the advance of old age, and, in consequence, the approach of death.

This linking together of death and the aged has its effect upon the emotional lives of the elderly. In a sense they are being constantly reminded of their own limited span of time. They are faced with the fact of their own mortality. There is a special and hideous kind of loneliness that can develop when you are an older person living in a strongly youth-oriented society. It is therefore important that if you are older, you do not allow yourself to be victimized by this ubiquitous philosophy. Although there is an increasing trend toward youth and youthfulness in this country, it does not need to become for you a path toward the grave. You can escape the loneliness that comes from feeling useless because of age by refusing to sit down and give up just because you have a certain number of chronological years left.

Mr. and Mrs. J., in their sixties, felt that none of their children needed them anymore, and they missed the activities they had enjoyed in their vigorous youth. Instead of sinking into the limbo of self-pitying, lonely lives, they applied to the Peace Corps and enrolled in a revitalizing training program. According to the last report, they were in Puerto Rico engaged is useful, stimulating work, happy and in good health, and much too busily occupied to think of being lonely.

If your community feels you have nothing to offer, then the burden of proof is upon you to show them that you do. The wisdom of years is a valuable gift to be shared with the young. If you genuinely wish to be committed to being a useful part of your community, no one will turn you away. A life dedicated to sharing and service leaves no room for being lonely.

4

When Loneliness Becomes a Way of Life

Many people who suffer constant loneliness seem in a strange way to have embraced their pain of isolation to a point of no return. Those who have succumbed to this degree feel fatigue of body and spirit as an everyday experience.

They may make some attempts to alleviate their condition, but they rarely do things that will have a lasting effect upon their loneliness. What they do is to engage in some dead-end activity that only helps them to use up a few minutes of their time. When that time is gone, they again succumb to feelings of misery and fatigue brought about by loneliness.

Some try to fill up the "silence" of being alone by playing a radio, or they attempt to live vicariously by watching television. Others call up their friends and have long telephone visits with them. But underneath any of these activities is the same gnawing loneliness, and for these people loneliness is a customary way of life.

If this is your experience, you not only feel blue but are probably also suffering from a series of minor physical illnesses which are, in effect, nothing more than disguised cries of self-pity from your unhappy soul.

It is a fact that loneliness and good health do not go together any more than do loneliness and happiness. The three—loneliness, good health, and happiness—cannot exist together on an equal basis in a personality. The lonely person listens to his own heartbeat, and what he hears is never good! He concentrates on himself because there is no one else in his life. That concentration on self gives rise to a host of minor but annoying physical ailments and complaints. The lonely person becomes a physically defective machine.

As a lonely person you might start to help yourself by checking into the relationship of your health to your loneliness. You may find, as I have seen in many cases, that the greater the loneliness, the poorer the health. How many of your health complaints are really valid? Would that headache disappear, for example, if someone asked you to go out to dinner? Or is your illness a defense against the hurt of not being asked to go out?

Whatever the exact psychological background of

your health problem, it is insidious in nature, for not only does it reflect your loneliness, but it contributes to it. We call such health problems psychosomatic illnesses. Psychosomatic is two words combined—"psyche," or "mind," and "soma," or "body." Together they stand for the close interrelationship of the two. You can talk yourself into an illness, and you can, because of loneliness, think yourself into not feeling well.

Saying that your illness is psychosomatic does not mean that you don't actually feel sick. You do, and you have pain and discomfort that are very real. That it is psychosomatic, however, *does* mean that the cause and cure are within yourself. No germ, allergy, or organic cause is responsible; it is your loneliness that is making you ill. Take care of the loneliness problem, and you will also take care of your health problem.

One of the difficulties with loneliness is that it becomes so overpowering with its influence, emotional gloom, physical disability, and mental sluggishness that you find it more and more difficult to escape—unless you make a concentrated effort.

I have observed that most lonely people put the burden of effort upon others to relieve their loneliness. They sit back and wait for that other person to make a gesture or take a step. That does not work, and unfortunately for the individual consumed with loneliness he sometimes cannot extricate himself from his misery if an opportunity does present itself. Has that ever happened to you? Does it happen frequently?

If it does, then perhaps when someone makes an overt effort to reach out to you, it seems just too much trouble to respond because of the shadow of gloom that hangs over your life. There is no lightness of spirit, no jubilation, no celebration of the sheer fact of existence. If you have allowed boredom to creep into all the corners of your daily life, there is no joy in awakening to the new day or any beauty to be found in sharing its surprises with others.

It *is* boring to be lonely. You are so preoccupied with physical and emotional complaints that there is no stimulation to life, and the sameness becomes suffocating. When you have reached that point, the next step is to rationalize the state of chronic loneliness.

The physical complaints we discussed above are one way in which you may rationalize your loneliness state. You say that you do not go out much because you suffer from chronic indigestion and most food does not agree with you. You *should* say that you don't get invited out to eat, and eating alone has given you chronic indigestion. You explain your not going to a concert on the grounds that you require a lot of sleep, and if you are out late at night, you are too tired the next day. In truth, you sleep because you have nothing else to do, and you don't want to go to the concert by yourself.

Sleeplessness, fatigue, ulcers, headaches, and even

colds can be caused by loneliness. Loneliness is a fertile breeding ground for physical and emotional symptoms.

Emotional symptoms coming from loneliness can be as disabling as physical ones. Moreover, emotional symptoms can also be used as a form of rationalization.

These emotional symptoms include fear, anger, self-pity, envy, and distrust. They, too, work very effectively to keep the lonely person isolated from others. The lonely person may say that he wants to be part of a group and form a lasting friendship with another person, but emotionally he has developed an unhealthy attitude of distrust and suspicion. This distrust and suspicion prevent him from accepting any overtures made to him by others. The lonely person who lets envy or hostility mask his loneliness has the same problem; he cannot relate successfully to other people.

Emotional symptoms, like physical ones, are barriers which, once erected, require a great effort of the will to break down. Life is too busy and too involved for most people to spend time trying to break down walls that you may have built; therefore, if the breach is to be made, it must be made from within. You will have to get out of your self-imposed prison of loneliness and make yourself available so that other people can get to know you.

The lonely person becomes his own enemy and eventually his own victim. All of these negative emotions and reactions about which we have been talking are things that feed the enemy. They are really unconsciously enjoyed and give impetus to the vicious cycle that pushes the victim further into himself. Sometimes that cycle becomes so deadly that the only way out seems to be suicide. And sometimes the lonely person makes a choice that is, on the surface at least, not so drastic and yet leads ultimately to the same end—death. A lonely person will often drink too much, eat too much, or smoke too much so that he deliberately courts death while escaping the onus of suicide.

Let's look at some of the ways in which other people have handled problems of loneliness. This may help you to make some decisions about your own loneliness problem. After all, loneliness is a condition that is common to millions of people throughout the world, and there are good and bad ways of handling it. Why not choose a good way to solve your loneliness problem?

Let's take John F., for example. John F. went from his work, which he found dull and unrewarding, to his home, where he felt bored and listless, and then back to work again. He spent his weekends in a drugged state of suspended activity, as if waiting for something to happen that was not to happen, or else he withdrew from the reality of his loneliness in extra hours of unneeded sleep.

He kept saying to himself how "out of it" he felt, but he did nothing to alter his treadmill existence. He suffered frequently from headaches and recurrent attacks of stomach ulcer. The headaches symbolized the feeling of gloom and dread that hung heavily over his head—just as the ulcer was tantamount to his gnawing angrily on his own stomach.

The description we have given of this man's mode of life would indicate that he was a solitary soul abiding in a vacuum, but this was not the case at all. The fact of the matter was that he was a teacher in the schools, in daily contact with hundreds of active, curious minds thirsty for knowledge and wisdom. A married man, his homelife was peopled by an attractive wife and three children. How could anyone be lonely with so many opportunities for sociability available and so many responsibilities to offer challenge? A situation of this kind would appear unbelievably absurd even for an unemployed person living alone and with no family.

But there was no absurdity in John's view of his desperate state of being. The reality was stark and terrifying. He looked upon his job as just a twice-a-month paycheck, not as an adventure in experiencing the mental and spiritual development of children. His responsibilities to his family were not looked upon as an exercise in shaping the next generation, but as a financial obligation that must be met.

How had he fallen so low in self-esteem as to see himself only as a machine for performing an endless procession of loathsome operations? Had he not at one time chosen a teaching career and planned it with enthusiasm, courted his wife, and looked forward to parenthood?

On close examination we see that here is a person fully capable of shaping his life according to plan, but where is the sense of accomplishment and fulfillment that should have followed as a natural reward? Why had John gradually become disillusioned and all his plans and dreams gone sour? The answer lies in his never really having given of himself—either to his vocation or to his marriage. He did all the required things but without any real sense of dedication or any feeling of enthusiasm or emotional investment. He accepted a robot's role—a mechanical man without emotional responses.

Teaching can be one of the most pleasurable of all occupations, but one must first reveal to the students the pride of possessing an inquisitive mind—the joy of questioning, exploring, and understanding any subject. For marriage to realize its full potential, its true depth and meaning, one must be willing to grow continually toward new levels of loving or at least to make the effort. There must be empathy with the marriage partner and a sharing of this effort, and as in all things conceived with good intentions and carried out with true devotion, the benefits are immeasurable, even though all goals may not be reached.

Children need much more from a father than food on the table and a roof overhead. The father of the family is the major model for manhood that children carry within them all through life. Fatherhood entails the giving of emotional time, sympathetic attention, and concerned discipline—the ingredients of loving and caring. But that is the very reason for bringing children into the world—to show them the best way one can live life fully and to share in the experience oneself.

It took a shattering encounter with death to shake John out of his lethargic loneliness. His accomplished younger brother was killed in a senseless accident. While sitting at the funeral, John kept thinking of the many times he had wished himself dead, of the complicated plans for suicide he had fantasied for making everyone realize how dreadfully they had treated him and causing them to suffer feelings of guilt and self-recrimination.

But John had not really wished himself dead, of course. What he had wanted was to be rescued from the death-in-life his life had become; suicide is the final solution to such loneliness. In thinking of the short time his brother had lived and how his brother's hopes and ambitions had been cut off prematurely in the prime of his youth, John was forced to confront himself with the pattern of his own life that gave nothing and dissolved only into emotions of self-pity. "What a silly waste!" he said.

With this shock of self-recognition began a slow psychological rebirth which was very difficult after so many years of avoiding involvement with others. But in spite of the difficulties, it is working. John is now beginning to feel an interest in his students, and this interest is projected onto his own children. He walks into his home with some willingness to give of himself, and his family has responded willingly and happily to his attempts to join them in emotional sharing.

"I wish I could change my life. I'm so miserable so much of the time!" Esther exclaimed in despair. She went on to say that whenever she had to be alone, she became nervous and depressed. Unfortunately for Esther her husband had to be gone several days each month on business. She would brood about her loneliness until she actually felt ill.

"I wish I had someone with me at those times," she said.

"You do" was my answer, and I wasn't being funny. Esther had herself. But Esther despised that self and was actually bored by her own personality. This was not surprising, since the personality she presented was that of a whining, self-centered, lonely person.

Esther could not change her life in the sense of changing her circumstances or her husband's work, but she could change her personality. She could learn to enjoy her own company and thus cope with a part of her loneliness. She could make herself over into someone who more closely resembled her ideal person, or as she put it, "I'd like to know someone who is interesting and creative."

Instead of sitting home feeling sorry for herself

when her husband was gone, Esther was persuaded to get out and do something that would be beneficial to her development as a person.

She had always been interested in local history but had never done anything to develop that interest. Now in an attempt to solve her loneliness problem and remake her personality. Esther joined the local historical society and became active in its campaign to preserve historical sites. Later she began to study local history and eventually went on to write a successful booklet about a Civil War battle in her home county.

From being a flat, one-dimensional personality, Esther became a full and rounded personality whom other people enjoyed meeting and being with; more important, Esther was no longer bored by herself, no longer lonely.

Marie N. had an experience similar to that of John F., and because of the death of a sister, she learned to reevaluate her own life in terms of her loneliness-induced despondency. A middle-aged woman, she had drifted away from her friends and family into a life that was devoid of any interest and companionship. She tried to excuse her loneliness by saying that at her age she couldn't expect to have "good times." And even though her loneliness made her terribly unhappy, she enjoyed it, for it was all that made her different from others—in her own eyes. It was an ugly plant that she nurtured and cared for with all of her concentration. But when her sister died after a short illness, Marie began to question her own life, and like John F., she saw that it had become a wasteland. She realized that loneliness had become a way of life for her, a kind of perverse enjoyment.

There should not have to be a traumatic experience such as confrontation with death in the family to cause a person to extricate himself from the quicksand of self-centered despair. Life is a precious gift, and we can all recognize and accept the fact that it is ours to experience to its fullest. One can be awed by it, extract joy from it, work with it, despair with its pain, glory in the beauty of its reality—but never, never waste it as if it will never end! Nor should one dwell in some dreamworld of the future, waiting out the fleeting present in the expectation of some magical change that will make things better later on.

It is really very sad to see someone who is continually postponing life. We all know that the only time that counts is the present, the "today" of our lives, yet most lonely people refuse to admit this.

Some lonely people sit around thinking about yesterdays and what used to be in their lives. They add to their loneliness by wishing that they could go back in time, that they could reproduce the scene and conditions of former years. Everything that has happened in the past is regarded with affection while the today world is looked upon with distaste.

If you have a tendency to look back at the past, you are not only cheating yourself out of life but also making your loneliness far worse than it really is.

You are denying yourself the chance to get over loneliness and start living.

If looking back is a form of escape that solves
nothing and adds to your burden, so also is looking
ahead in the hope and anticipation that through no
effort of your own, life will be changed for you. Loneliness is not like the weather. It does not vanish with
the sun. You yourself have to eradicate it from your
life.

Being lonely and wishing that something or someone would just happen along to take away that loneliness is futile. Just as frogs do not change into princes
or sleeping princesses wait for that magic kiss, so
there is no magic formula to banish loneliness.

Only you, the lonely person, can make the change
in your life. Yes, you can sit around either looking
back or looking forward, but these things only increase your loneliness. You can spend your life thumb-
ing through old snapshots or waiting for that knock
on the door, until the only thing left is your old age
and then death.

Life ends in death, and what you do with it in the
interim is your privilege and your responsibility. People who give in to loneliness act as if they will have
forever to enjoy this special suffering. How can this
be possible when we see the dying process around
us continually? What makes the human animal so
perverse as to devise so many ways to deny his short
time on this earth?

What aspect of yourself convinces you that it is

useless to attempt any positive change? Where does this great physical tiredness and emotional lassitude that keeps you a prisoner of loneliness originate? When you make a slight effort to give of yourself, upon what storehouse of pessimism do you draw that makes the attempt so faint and feeble?

We all seem to have a perverse streak in our natures, some distortion in mental structure, that derives satisfaction from keeping friendly, satisfying things from happening to us. Take the case of Lenore.

At a discussion club Lenore sees an attractive man, obviously alone, struggling with his coat, all twisted in the sleeves. She *wants* to do the natural, thoughtful thing—offer to help him with his coat, perhaps beginning a conversation . . . a friendship . . . who knows? That is the excitement of life—not knowing what will happen but going ahead and letting the drama unfold.

A voice in Lenore's inner self says, "Oh, don't offer to help him—he'll just laugh at you." So she sets aside her natural impulses and feels even more left out. Her little voice promises what? That she will be laughed at for making a generous gesture, but it offers nothing as an alternative!

This part of the mind is usually operating unconsciously, but it is nonetheless quite real and extremely effective. It is a self-put-down device and should at all times be questioned. It controls our actions subtly and swiftly, directing our responses so that we are hardly aware of its restrictions. This safeguard of our naturally generous, outgoing impulses makes us behave with such caution and prudence that it destroys our joy in living and is, in reality, not a protecting angel at all, but a dangerous enemy. It represents a complex system of prohibitions known as the unconscious superego and works its spell against the forces of joy, love, and fulfillment. It seriously restrains our freedom of will and holds us prisoners.

We are afraid of letting go because we do not have sufficient trust in ourselves. Through the years we have built up this elaborate system which, although it is intended to be a safeguard, turns out to be a trap for loneliness. By way of contrast watch a room full of children, and see how they react on interpersonal levels. They have no inhibitions in expressing themselves. They play together, and if so inclined, they share. In a given period of time they may show sympathy, affection, dislike, and irritation, but always there is interest in one another. On the other hand, adults placed in a group will not react with the same freedom of expression. They are guarded in their interpersonal responses. They exhibit varying degrees of friendliness and will often turn away in embarrassment from any display of emotion. They appear to be under the influence of some power greater than their own wills. They remain isolated in their own pools of loneliness. Is that an accurate picture of you when you are part of a group? Do you feel compelled to maintain your loneliness as if it had some power over your life?

If your answer is Yes, you can overcome this power if you allow the messages to come through that urge you to break out of your shell of noninvolvement. How can you do this? One way is to ask yourself some pertinent questions about your life—about your loneliness and your inability to become personally involved with other people and other issues. Why are you afraid of involvement? Is there really any sound basis for your inhibitive actions? You should look at your life and see if this pattern of noninvolvement is based on an unwillingness on your part or on an emotional inability to approach other people.

An unwillingness implies a conscious act and a deliberate one. You could become involved, but you have conditioned yourself not to respond to other people. This problem should be handled by attempting to discover the behind-the-scenes cause of your alienation. Your attitude may come from some traumatic childhood or adolescent experience which you have magnified out of proportion and thus allowed to become a dominant influence in your adult life.

One of my patients, Grace, was lonely and bored and like Lenore was unable to respond warmly toward other individuals. She admitted that she knew why she reacted this way. "I had a very close friend when I was a teen-ager," she said, "but one day I discovered that my friend had not only told classmates some secret things I had told her, but she also made fun of me. In fact, I caught her giving an imitation of my voice and the way I used my hands!" Grace's tone was still bitter, although the incident to which she referred had happened some twenty years before. She had to realize that she was condemning herself to a life of adult misery and loneliness because of a thoughtless act by a friend during adolescence. Grace had also to learn that not all friends would behave in this way and that she was, through her own stubbornness, shutting herself out of a big part of life. She gradually learned to be more friendly, to go out of her way to appear interested in people. It was not easy for her to learn to prefer the company of others instead of wallowing in her loneliness, but in time she did change her attitude toward other people.

An inability to become involved may be the signal of some severe emotional or psychological problem that will require professional help or consultation. However, if you suffer from this inability to respond, you can try to make changes in your life and see if you cannot conquer this social disability.

You must first convince yourself of the importance of making meaningful contacts with others. After this first step you must take the second—the actual act of some form of contact. One man I know resolved that he would say "Good morning" to anyone he met on his way to work. At first this proved to be all that he could bring himself to do, but in a few weeks he broadened this to include a few words of conversation with the neighborhood grocer and then others. He also made a conscious effort to be more friendly to his co-workers and as a result discovered that he had a number of things in common with other people. Soon he was participating in a hiking and camera club and enjoying other social activities. His days of loneliness were over, because he had conquered his seeming inability to reach out toward others.

You can do something very similar with your loneliness problem. Start on a small scale; let things develop slowly and naturally. Join a church group, or an adult education class, or get involved in some kind of volunteer work. It is not so important what you do but the cooperative spirit with which you do it.

Don't be afraid to make that friendly gesture toward a stranger—a stranger who may be as lonely as you are. If you see a person who is in need of some assistance, don't be like Lenore—afraid of giving. Do what you can to help, even if it is something as simple as assisting with a coat. It is the gesture of openness that is important. What you are doing is giving something of yourself to others, and when you do that, you do not lose—you gain in self-esteem. The more self-esteem you build up, the easier it is for you to act positively. You will become noticeably less lonely, because you have a new and better self-concept of your personality.

You can change your whole life once you are able to disregard the voice of censorship that holds you always in fear that you'll do the wrong thing, the foolish thing, the imprudent, impractical thing that is going to make you look silly and ridiculous. Long practice at listening to these unconscious fears has conditioned you mentally so that you have built up an actual need to be lonely, and this is a mental habit that is not easily overcome. You are not going to win the battle every time you fight the unconscious attraction to loneliness, which draws you like a magnet even as you try to resist, but the attempt itself is a step in a positive direction.

Because of its dark and shadowy nature, the self-condemning part of the mind is elusive. More on its nature and how to cope with it will follow. But an increasing portion of life can be wonderful if you are willing to challenge this enemy. What are you losing if you don't always keep in mind that this moment, this day—*your* day—will pass and never return?

What will you do with this unique gift?

5

Escaping Instead of Solving

"Don't cry, Julie. Here, have a cookie."

Have you ever witnessed such a scene? Since most adults feel uncomfortable when confronted by tears, they hurry to stop them by any means, including bribery. From a psychological point of view it would be better if Julie were permitted to cry. If allowed to express herself in this way, there is a good chance she will discover the real cause of her tears and learn a lesson invaluable for reaching maturity.

Instead, most adults follow the behavior pattern that is most familiar to them and try to distract the crying child by offering a substitute. They make no attempt to discover why the tears and work back toward a solution of the problem. Giving a distressed or frightened child a cookie, a piece of candy, or a toy sets an unfortunate and unrealistic precedent. The child learns to postpone the "reckoning of accounts," an attitude that can be a serious handicap in adulthood.

The lesson is that there are solutions to problems if you are free to express your feelings concerning them and to talk about them with someone else. Whatever may be causing the distress, talking about it and actively seeking some answers is the most effective way of overcoming the difficulty. Too often parents take the easy way out by diverting the child's attention from his problems. This is a grave disservice to a growing personality. The cookie ploy is only a palliative and not a cure; it merely shows the child how to escape sadness by the use of infantile (oral) means of resolution.

The adult who has been bribed into escape as a child carries this attitude into adulthood. As a result we see such cases as the wife who cries when confronted by a domestic problem. She expects and knows that her husband will do anything to stop those tears. A man will not usually cry when faced with an intolerable situation or frustration; he may instead escape into some other activity which postpones facing the real issue.

Loneliness as a common social and personality problem may result in childish attempts at escape rather than in work at solving the problem. Take the Julie at the beginning of this chapter; suppose that we now have an older Julie, a widow, and she is crying because she is lonely since the death of her husband. What she wants now in response to her tears is not a cookie but another person to look after her, to help her with decisions, and to accompany her when she goes to social events. The principle is the same, however, and if Julie the child was conditioned to expect a cookie or other diversion in times of personal stress, Julie the adult is also going to expect some happy and convenient escape from her problem.

This would work only if there were "super-adults" who were *in loco parentis* to all adults. The truth is, as Julie the adult will have to learn, we adults are responsible for ourselves and have to take action to help ourselves. This is not to say that there are no helping hands—there are, both professional and amateur—but the main effort lies with the individual. Julie the widow will have to do what Julie the child never had to do—look at the reason for her tears and then look for the solution.

Let's look at the case of Louise H., who said: "I don't know what's the matter with me! I feel so blue and have so much trouble with my digestion. I guess I inherited a poor stomach because my father always had trouble with his digestion."

What Louise had "inherited" was not poor digestion but loneliness and inability to confront her problems. As a child she had been spared any stress by her indulgent parents. When she failed to make friends, she was told that it was because the other children were jealous of her charm and clothes. As an adult Louise was lonely because she did not know how to reach out to other people. Instead of facing the fact of her own personality inadequacy and taking steps to correct it, Louise blamed her depression on her digestion. And her digestive problems were the physical symptom of her emotional condition, not the cause of it.

You may, like Louise, consciously say that you do not understand why you are upset and depressed, but unconsciously you have the desire to express your unhappiness. Louise said, "I have a digestion problem" when she really wanted to say, "I have a loneliness problem."

The lonely person frequently responds in a childish way because he does not know any other response. Even when he does not actually break down and cry because of his frustration, he may do other things which are on an emotional level with crying.

In studies of alcoholics the basic personality is invariably that of a childish person who cannot face life without his liquor crutch. He is not any different from the frightened and unhappy child who is comforted by the offer of a cookie. The alcoholic "mothers" himself by popping the bottle into his mouth in response to insecurity and frustration.

As we have already shown, there are many people who frankly admit they began drinking because of being lonely. Booze is no solution to the problem of loneliness. It has the reverse effect of causing the person to withdraw even further into a vague and hazy world of his own, automatically shutting off any opportunities for companionship. The same applies for the heavy user of drugs.

The experience of Carl was not unusual. A minor and overworked executive in a large company, Carl was a lonely man. He lived alone and had no close friends or relatives. In an effort to get away from his loneliness he turned to alcohol. In his case it was the most convenient way to forget his problem of loneliness. Had he been in a different culture group, he might have turned to drugs or even something as apparently innocuous as food. In Carl's social circle free time was frequently spent at cocktail parties, so there was always the availability of alcohol.

By the time Carl realized what he was doing to himself he had become thin, nervous, and worried about his future—both with the company and with himself.

"I don't think I can go on like this," he said. "I'm beginning to despise myself to the extent that I sometimes think I would be better off dead! When I started drinking, it was just to be one of the crowd. I only took one or two, and while I was drinking and around people, life seemed to have more meaning and I felt less lonely. Well, since liquor seemed to have a relaxing effect, I started drinking when I was alone, but it didn't really help my loneliness."

Carl had used alcohol to give himself a false sense of belonging, but the effect did not last. Finally he was drinking more and more and yet becoming socially less desirable. Drinking, instead of giving him the fellowship of others, was cutting him off from people. It was putting him in isolation.

"I'm twice as miserable and lonely now," he said, "but I don't seem to be able to stop."

With help Carl broke out of the vicious circle in which he had trapped himself. He joined his local Alcoholics Anonymous group for assistance in overcoming his dependence on alcohol. He also looked for a way to cure his loneliness. This he did by becoming involved in helping others at the community center for disadvantaged boys and girls. As a former basketball star in high school and college Carl was able to put that past to work in a positive way by coaching the boys' basketball team. Being useful gave Carl the feeling of acceptance that he needed to get over his loneliness.

Why was Alcoholics Anonymous also a help to Carl? Alcoholics Anonymous is a successful organization composed of individuals who themselves have experienced the desolation of alcoholism and recognize the despair and loneliness of the heavy drinker. The program is specifically oriented toward creating a social atmosphere by emphasizing the values of human contact. No matter where an A.A. meeting occurs, there is a helpful, genuine family feeling. By means of identification with a problem that is mutually shared, a real feeling of comradeship results—without regard to social or financial differences or whether the participants come from Texas or Vermont. All barriers are self-dissolving as a common problem is laid bare and its solution sought without shame or excuse but only an admission of need. This family of persons is dedicated to giving help to others suffering from the same affliction.

If your lonely life is further complicated by a drinking problem, don't waste valuable years trying to rationalize whether you're really an alcoholic or only a "social drinker." You already have your answer. You have nothing to lose by dropping in on an A.A. meeting (places where these meetings are being held are posted conspicuously in most communities and listed in the general directory of your telephone book). Instead, you have much to gain. In place of a befuddled brain, loss of self-esteem, and an exorbitant amount of money sloshed down an unsatisfied throat, you have the companionship of people who wish you well without offering condemnation, and you have so much to recover in self-respect. Soon you will be helping a "new boy" yourself, and with this challenge to sustain you, you certainly won't be lonely anymore.

What about the drug-user? An individual may say that he uses drugs because he wants to deepen his experience or enlarge his perceptions, but he is actually using drugs because he is lonely. He prefers to rationalize about his use of drugs rather than admit that he is a failure in human relationships or a failure at living with himself.

Drugs are not an answer to loneliness, for they only compound the alienation, the loneliness, of the user.

Putting aside any questions of either the morality of drugs or the effect upon health, the drug addict is wrong because using drugs causes him to drift further away from the shore of reality, a shore he would like very much to reach if he knew how to do it.

Of course, drinking and drugs are the most obvious of the negative responses to loneliness, but there are others, and one of the most common is overeating. Overeating, like drinking, is linked directly to the inability of an adult to respond to problems in an adult way. Alcohol and food are typical babyish responses. They are the adult answer to the cry for "Mama" and the reach for the nipple. Unfortunately they do not satisfy an adult in the same way a baby or small child is satisfied with some oral token. A lonely adult cannot escape, except momentarily, through his oral satisfactions.

Mrs. K. was a lonely woman, and she was a fat woman, for she had become a constant eater. She admitted that she used food in an attempt to cheer herself up. This form of emotional dependence on food is not unusual nor is it confined to any one age group. Lonely children will overeat; so will lonely adolescents, lonely adults, and lonely old people.

The hunger pains that Mrs. K. felt were really hunger pains for love and companionship. She was trying to induce a feeling of well-being and happiness in her life by eating. But her obesity was causing her unhappiness, for she felt that she was conspicious by her size.

"I'm ashamed to face my acquaintances," she said. "But I get depressed and then I eat and then I'm depressed again!"

Mrs. K. had to get out of her own trap just as Carl did, and when she was able to take the step toward a more meaningful life, she was able to cut down on her eating. She actually lost weight because she was too busy helping others. She no longer had time to sit around, brood, and eat more than she needed.

As we pointed out in Chapter 3, illness is another common response to loneliness. The lonely individual becomes unduly preoccupied with his own health because he has to do something to try to fill up the void of an empty life. But illness can never be the same as friendships and contacts with other people. It does not solve the loneliness problem; rather it aggravates it, since few people want to listen to the complaints of another person.

Hypochondria, a morbid preoccupation with one's own state of health, will drive people away from you instead of attracting them. You will get indifference instead of sympathy. Certainly you will not get love.

Are any of these negative responses to loneliness the ones you have chosen as your own? Is this the best that you can do for yourself? These negative responses to loneliness are not adult ones. They show a lack of emotional and intellectual maturity. Why do you find it necessary to act in such a childish fashion?

Out of their relative helplessness and inexperience children look to their parents to solve their problems for them. A wise parent encourages the child to help himself as much as possible, even if it means making some mistakes. What is learned from trial-and-error experimentation helps to develop habits of independence. Although it is appropriate that parents help children with problems that are beyond their ability to solve, unfortunately many parents keep their children so dependent that when they enter adulthood, they look for substitute parents to lean on for the solution to their problems: the school, the boss, the government—these are examples of Mom and Dad taking care of all the problems that are encountered in life's arena.

This kind of dependency is projected into every phase of adult life. People who operate Lonely Hearts Clubs use it to exploit lonely persons, and through deceptive advertising they promise (for a fee) to arrange a meeting with a compatible stranger (for a fee) as a solution to all those lonely evenings.

The advertisement suggests that your childlike incompetence makes it imprudent, if not impossible, for you to go out on your own and meet new people. A machine, presumably, can do a better job through its programming devices of judging who your friends and associates should be. So (for a fee), all arrangements are made down to the last detail.

Why has the computer-arranged date become so

popular? Why have so many lonely people been willing to put their trust in an impersonal machine? The computer with its wires, transistors, blinking lights, and many electronic components has become the new matchmaker. One reason is that in today's highly technological society people have a tendency to put their faith in machines rather than in people. They feel that a machine will be impartial and unbiased and won't cheat them. They forget that with every machine there is a human operator!

Let's take a closer look at this supposedly infallible means of locating happiness and a marriage partner. First, computer selection is a very expensive proposition to the client. The cost can run as high as one thousand dollars, the average cost being about five hundred dollars. This is in great contrast to the costs of the first computer courtship clubs which charged five to ten dollars. However, when interest in computer dates grew, the operators of such clubs realized that they had the makings of big business on their hands, and prices rose suddenly and astronomically.

Second, although some computer dating bureaus are honest and do attempt to furnish the services they advertise, a good many of them have been proved to be frauds. Attorney General Louis Lefkowitz, of New York, investigated at least one hundred cases where clients had never received the services they had paid for.

Other government investigators have found that in some cases dating bureaus did not even own or use a computer to match up clients, although their advertising specifically stated that computers were used. Complaints by dissatisfied and disillusioned clients included such things as being introduced to persons not suitable or compatible in terms of common interests and backgrounds. One woman said that she received an obscene proposal from the man sent to her by the agency she consulted. Another client said that although she had been promised that she would meet only professional men of a specified height and age, she was introduced to nonprofessional men of varying heights and ages.

It is because of this large number of complaints that consumer-minded officials would like to see the states enact some form of stricter legal control over all kinds of dating and matchmaking services and clubs.

Yes, some clients are happy with dates obtained from computer dating bureaus, but they are among the fortunate and happy minority. Generally speaking, there have been more people disappointed and frustrated with this attempt to solve their loneliness problem than those pleased and rewarded. Sometimes this disenchantment is the fault of the service, which may be a shoddy operation in which no real attempt is made to match up personality traits scientifically. But computer dating can also be a failure for psychological reasons, which have to do with the problems of the people who enlist those services in the first place.

Even the most reputable and honest computer dating service cannot cope with misrepresentation by its clients. Some individuals provide false information about themselves. Many people who use dating bureaus are defensive about themselves, their personalities, their hopes, education, professions, and interests. Men will often lie about their jobs and educational attainments. Women tend to lie about their ages and physical statistics as well as their interests. These lies are usually not outright attempts at fraud but the reflection of emotional problems. What these individuals are doing is providing the dating bureau with information about personalities they wish they possessed. Not only are they looking for some escape from loneliness, but they are hoping for some magic that will give them the personalities and lives they have invented.

As one man explained, "I said I was a doctor and had graduated from a well-known university, even though I was a mechanic. I wanted to lead a different life, and I thought that maybe if I met the right person, my life would be the way I had always dreamed it could be."

Computer services or any other form of arranged companionship won't solve either problems of personality adjustment or loneliness. They are ways of attempting to evade reality.

The entire proceeding is humiliating and ordinarily far from satisfactory; the fantasy of meeting the "right" person under these circumstances instantly dissolves when, in reality, you are introduced to just another dependent, lonely person like yourself who is looking for a mother or father to lean on. However, this time Mom and Dad have attached a price tag on the glittering promises that comprise their stock in trade.

There was the case of one of our acquaintances who had considered the possible advantages of joining such a club, even though she was skeptical about someone else being more competent than herself in picking her friends for her. She decided to talk it over with us before taking any definite steps.

"Might there not be some other way for you to meet interesting people of your own age?" we asked her. (Ethel was at that time about fifty-eight.) "Had you ever thought about doing your own advertising?"

Well, this was exactly what she did. She was careful to avoid the negative "I am lonely—help me" approach. She posted a notice in the weekly bulletin of a church near her home, which read: "Do you like children? Are your grandchildren living far away from you? How about joining a group of people interested in becoming foster grandparents? We need grandmothers and grandfathers! Let's make baby-sitting a personal experience for the child and the sitter!" She asked her grocer to let her put up the notice in his store. She also obtained permission from the manager of a nearby apartment building to place an ad in the foyer. Most of the people who lived there were of the fifty-to-seventy age group.

In a few weeks the idea began to catch on. People were at first reluctant to admit they were lonely and starved for companionship, but soon the word got around about how much fun everyone was having at the small gatherings at the homes of the members, showing off their foster charges and exchanging recipes and fishing stories. Obviously Ethel's problem was solved, but more important, by initiating a program of group involvement, a solution was found for many other people whose loneliness was just as great as her own.

All these people, acting independently, were able to find a truly constructive solution for dispelling their lonely existences and bringing happiness to themselves and others. They were able to meet a great many more people—the mothers and fathers of the children as well as persons of both sexes of their own age group—than they would have done by subscribing to the computerized services of a Lonely Hearts Club. Instead of spending money in futile searches and embarrassed frustration, they were actually able to earn money as paid baby-sitters.

In Los Lunas, New Mexico, there is a state home for retarded children that has successfully used a program of adoptive grandparents. Older persons of the community give a few hours a day playing with and loving the children. Institution personnel have found the program to be a valuable aid in getting better responses from the children. In addition, it has proved to be of help to the older person serving as a grandparent, for he or she no longer feels lonely and unwanted. As one "grandmother" told me: "It has given me real purpose in my life. I used to feel so lonely and sorry for myself because my children and grandchildren lived so far away. My physical health is better now, too, because I know there are others who need me."

Any kind of volunteer or service program can help you get over that lonely, useless feeling. There are plenty of opportunities for you to help others, and in so doing you will find that you have also helped yourself.

We have been talking about some of the more common forms of escape from loneliness—alcoholism and turning to dating bureaus and similar attempts to find a quick and easy solution. There are other ways in which you may be trying to avoid facing yourself and your loneliness. Some are as obvious as taking drugs, overeating, and surrounding yourself with people. But other ways may not appear to you to be possible escape routes, and yet that is what they are. If you tire easily and require lots of rest and sleep, the real answer may be your loneliness problem. Sleeping is one way people have of getting away from loneliness. Not only are they unaware of their frustrating loneliness when they are asleep, but their dreams may be more interesting than their waking lives.

I have known a number of persons who would have denied that they were lonely, yet the many hours of sleep they required indicated a form of escapism. Sleeping is pleasant. It is warm and acts like an anesthetic so that you can forget your problem of loneliness. However, as soon as you wake up, open your eyes, and become fully conscious, the helpless feeling of loneliness is right where you left it—inside of yourself.

Excessive daydreaming is another escape route, but it, too, provides a false life only for a period of time. The lonely young girl who daydreams of a handsome lover and a gay social time is doubly lonely when she comes out of her reverie and finds her life untouched by her romantic fancies and therefore unchanged.

The reality of your loneliness problem is always more potent than the brief magic of your sleeping dreams or your waking daydreams.

Frequent accidents or an emphasis on physical disabilities is a common way of attempting to cover up extreme loneliness. It is another way of trying to escape from the unpleasant facts of life. Many an individual tries to disguise the loneliness of his existence by claiming that in any case he is unable to take part in normal social activities. Actually his disability would vanish in a minute if he could be granted his secret wish—the opportunity to be with others.

Jane excused her empty social life by saying that a limp she had as a result of a childhood accident made it impossible for her to engage in normal social activities. The older Jane got, the more she withdrew, and the greater her limp became. Soon people were taking her at her own value, and they ceased to invite her out, since she claimed that any form of exercise was too tiring.

The loneliness that Jane suffered was needless. Had she concentrated on developing her personality, she would have had no problem in making and keeping friends. From a physical point of view her disability was so slight that it would not have kept her from any form of activity.

The lonely person is a desperate person, and he looks for the easiest way to justify his loneliness. He also looks for the quickest way to try to cover up that loneliness. It can be done in any of the ways we have been discussing. It can be done by trying to get lost in a crowd. The whole trouble is that none of these methods will work. Loneliness is like a boomerang: It keeps coming back. You can't throw it away; you have to really get rid of it.

Lonely people are frequently lazy people—lazy in the sense that they want things to happen to them, to be done for them. They don't want to work at solving their loneliness. They want it to disappear for them without any effort on their part. One way they try is to surround themselves with lots of other people but always on a superficial level.

It is easy to get into the cocktail circuit where conversation is as skimpy as the hors d'oeuvres. People will spend three minutes in shallow chatter with the person on the barstool beside them before sliding off to the next ear. This kind of social encounter tends to prohibit the flowering of a meaningful social relationship. It is only a momentary escape and no solution at all.

Yet people try to convince themselves that they are making a positive effort to do something about their loneliness problem by getting out and mixing with other people. But this kind of rationalizing solves nothing if it means only getting caught up in an impersonal, misdirected group of people who are doing exactly the same thing! Such relationships are without substance and are only a vacuous waste of life.

Do you feel anxious if you are not constantly surrounded by other people? Instead of burying yourself in hordes of uninterested people, try being alone with yourself to see if you can discover the secret of overcoming anxieties by means of meditation. This is something that can never be accomplished in the jazzy, flittering aura of a no-talk cocktail party. Physical relaxation while you listen to your thoughts and the biddings of your unconscious mind can bring great spiritual comfort and serenity which gradually supplant the frustrating need to be with other people all the time.

Practice self-awareness. Consider your own self-worth. Walt Whitman exulted in the riches of his own being in "Song of Myself," which begins:

I celebrate myself, and sing myself,
And what I assume you shall assume,

For every atom belonging to me as good as be-
  longs to you.

I loafe and invite my soul,
I lean and loafe at my ease observing a spear of
  summer grass.

Think of all the ways of building up your sense of
personal worth, your self-esteem, and do it in relationship to your value to yourself and to others.

You can build up your self-esteem by having some
therapeutic sessions with yourself. It may help if you
sit down and list on paper some of the facts about
yourself and your life. One of your troubles may be
that you are selling yourself short! Have a thorough
but realistic reappraisal of your achievements and
your capabilities. List the things you have accomplished, things for which you rightly deserve recognition and praise. Too many people are confused into
thinking that an achievement to be notable must be
of some tremendous world importance. This is not
true. The real hallmark of achievement is not in the
deed itself but in the doing of it. The housewife who
becomes a good cook and the man who becomes
proficient in his trade, whatever it is, have the right
to consider themselves worthy of self-recognition.
Success as a person is not necessarily the same as
public success. As a part of your self-awareness program you should learn to be aware of your successes
and let them raise your self-esteem.

Only when you are aware of your true worth as a person can you convey that sense of personality to others. If you have a low opinion of yourself, you will not find it easy to acquire and keep friends. You will be lonely. But when you know who you are, when you like yourself, then you will have something to give others. Being attractive to others is a matter of personality, not physical features.

Where do you begin? We have already discussed the need to try to change those qualities in yourself that you find unpleasant and to recognize that other people must find them even more so. But you will need to test how well you have succeeded. You can best gauge the degree of self-improvement by the way other people respond to the "new" you.

If you are interested in card-playing, there are groups willing to accept new members. You don't have to be an expert. There is usually a niche for a learner just as there is for an experienced player. Although card-playing is a wedge for becoming a member of a social group and a good springboard for initiating friendships, it should not be the primary reason for maintaining the social relationship. It is a pleasant form of relaxation, but don't hide behind the game as if excusing the real reason for seeking friends. You should never be ashamed to admit an honest need for people, for their friendship. Once the cards are put away, how will you project yourself as a member of the group by initiating other occasions for being together?

Having a recreation or a hobby in common is something familiar to lean upon as a beginning of a personal relationship, but it is a flimsy thread to hang a lasting friendship upon. Still, it makes extending oneself a bit easier. After all, you are reading this book to find some solutions for a very universal problem—that happens to be your individual problem only as it fits your own experience. But loneliness is no respecter of persons or station in life.

You need to act in some specific way to alter the conditions that happen to be the source of your loneliness. With someone else the conditions may be very different. If you don't know how to play bridge (or whatever game is seasonally popular in your locality), make the effort to learn. That is *one* condition, then, that can be marked off the list of your reasons for being lonely.

Where to go? The church is waiting, always there, with people hoping to share a bond of trust in a community. More than any other institution, churches absorb all ages, so it makes no difference if you are young or old, single, married, widow, or widower—there are others of identical status you will find in a church group to communicate with. Again, honest self-examination is essential before you attempt to relate to others.

What are you interested in? Do you have a lively curiosity about people and events? Or have you allowed your interest to be consumed by your problems so that you have become only self-centered? Do you want to share your mind and your ideas with others? Then why not start a reading and discussion group?

Remember, someone has to give the first smile, utter the opening word to begin a conversation, extend the hand that invites a friendship. Why shouldn't it be you? Does that small put-down voice inside direct you to wait for the other person to initiate these ice-breaking moves? It is generally true that if you want to be wanted by others, you must be willing to let them know it by giving first. As for that voice that says, "Hold back—let someone else make the first gesture," your answer should be "No, I'll be the one to venture forth with hope instead of waiting back like a timid child for someone to notice and bring me a cookie."

You will feel proud for having actively set aside your timidity and overcome your fears so that you can push yourself into opportunities for social fulfillment. That pride gives you the courage to extend yourself further. The first attempt is always the hardest, but the next time is easier. Gradually you will overcome the feeling of self-consciousness and any anxiety you may have about appearing forward or pushy. And suppose you should occasionally be shunned for making an outgoing gesture that is misunderstood: Isn't it better to have built up your self-confidence so that you were able to venture so far? That is an accomplishment in itself! A warm word is never spoken amiss—just remember that—and people who are worth your caring about will agree. You can just tell yourself, "This barrier is not my problem," and move on to the next adventure. You might even stop to feel some sympathy for those who are too frightened to accept your attempts at friendliness. You should understand, for you were once just as frightened.

CHAPTER

6

The Scene of Battle

Donald awoke to the sound of birds singing their morning serenade. He wandered into his kitchenette, looked out the window, and felt the beauty of the new day. The sun rising over the mountains in the distance cast dark shafts and pink rays into the pale morning sky. Poets of the eighteenth century, reveling as they did in the wonders of outdoor nature, described this phenomenon as the "rosy-fingered dawn." Even today in Hungary there is a saying that if you rise early enough to witness this scene of celestial grandeur, you become a part of the morning yourself, as nature intended.

Donald was a free-lance writer in his late twenties. He had worked for different newspapers and agencies in many places in the country. He had lived in large cities and made good money, but he was always unhappy. Although he was a man who enjoyed companionship, he was still unmarried, hoping to find the girl with whom to share his life. There was no question of the sincerity of his desire, but he never seemed to have the energy to pursue it. He asked himself why he felt so worn out all the time, and thus began an exercise in self-analysis as he reviewed the pattern of his days.

First, from having read an article about dreams, he realized that the constant excess of noise in a big city prevents city dwellers from ever having a good night's sleep. Yes, he slept, but not the deep, healing sleep that rejuvenates the body and spirit for the day ahead. After a night's fitful slumber he would arise unrefreshed, his view of the world clouded by smog, buildings with flashing lights, and the din from traffic and industry obscuring any other sounds that might be pleasing to the ear.

There was nothing of nature's beauty to soothe the senses. Donald was aware that these environmental blights were undermining his joy of living. On the way to work he was frustrated by the daily traffic jams that never seemed to unravel, and his nerves were bombarded by the honking of horns and screeching of tires. Tense with anxiety that he would be late for work, his already unrefreshed spirit was exhausted by the time he arrived at his desk.

With all these negative aspects of daily existence to drain off a person's energy and well-being, it can be readily seen that the ability to relate in a warm, human way to others would be sorely tried. These intrusions are called ego impingements.

Noise, population density, and pollution, all of which cause tension, are factors that result in ego impingement. The ego is the conscious part of the mind. It is a basic component of the personality and is the part most directly affected by environment. If the environment is mainly negative in nature, this will have an adverse effect upon the ego. When there is constant assault by adverse factors, impingement may take place to such a degree that the levels of awareness and perception drop. Constant impingement means a gradual and permanent wearing away of areas of sensitivity. The battered city dweller acquires a shell that protects him both physically and emotionally, and although this may decrease his vulnerability, it also decreases his wholesome involvement in life. This dulling of emotional response adds to the individual's personal loneliness.

With only so much energy to expend, if one has to use it to defend himself from noise, ugliness, bad sights, and smells, there will not be much left for working, creating, and loving. Stagnant water left in a vase affords no refreshment to a bouquet of flowers.

The people Donald dealt with at work, having experienced identical traumas, were in no way helpful— not even pleasant or friendly. They, too, were burdened by the same anxieties to get through the workday, get the job done, and serve whatever time was stipulated for earning all that "great" money that was supposed to make it all worthwhile.

A stranger to our planet and culture might come to the erroneous conclusion that the problems of big-city living could lead to an intensity of sharing and mutual commiseration and understanding among people. Unfortunately this is not true. That is why loneliness is such a problem in the cities.

"I feel so lost and alone," Muriel complained. "I live in an apartment house that has more people than my original hometown, but nobody has time to speak to anyone, or maybe they're afraid to speak. They don't want to get involved."

Muriel had become so tense that she had recurring dreams in which she was taken ill and was unable to summon help and assistance from her neighbors. "I thought they passed by my open door and still didn't hear my cries for help," she said in recounting one of her dreams.

It was hard for her to realize that people no longer have an interest in what happens to their neighbors. A cry for help usually goes unanswered, and any plea for assistance is usually ignored, if not scorned. Muriel had discovered that in the large city most people reserve their concern and interest for their own immediate circle of friends or family members. Others remain unknown and really do not exist as individuals.

Both Muriel and Donald had discovered that the large salaries they received did not in any way compensate for the loneliness they felt. Both of them spoke of the abrupt and cold transition from home to office. "It's not that people are so wonderful or so outgoing at work," Muriel explained, "but at least there are people there who know who you are. I leave work, and from then on I am generally surrounded by strangers who are indifferent to me. This goes on until I make the effort to get together with friends. I don't have friends in the area where I live, so it requires some planning to get together. After a hard day's work I am too tired, and so are my friends, to plan anything very extensive."

As for Donald, he would brave his way back to his gritty apartment building, worn out and ready to begin another night's battle with the restless stupor that passed for sleep.

By his own assessment of the situation Donald concluded that he wasn't going to solve his state of lonely desperation as long as he remained under constant environmental attack. He argued with himself that if he should move to another place, a small community with fewer ego impingements, he would have to satisfy himself with a smaller paycheck. But if he enjoyed no personal satisfaction and derived no pleasure from his well-paid job, what was the advantage of it? Just how many meals can one person eat in a single day? All that's needed is one chair to sit in, and you can't wear more than one outfit of clothing at a time.

Donald had traveled extensively. He remembered a

place in Colorado where the air was clean, the sky
clear, and the surroundings breathtakingly beautiful.
He began to toy with the idea of seeking employment
in such a place. The thought of making a change ex-
cited him. He could hardly wait to put his affairs in
order and set out on what he now looked upon as an
important adventure. He was determined to act.
After all, there was nothing of importance to be
gained by staying!

The job Donald found not only paid less money but
also carried less status and, correspondingly, less
responsibility. He was surprised to find that living
in a small town is far less expensive, though, than in
a large city and that it didn't seem to matter whether
he drove a Ford or a Cadillac. There seemed to be a
sincere interest in one's fellow workers and enough
time and energy to express it in the exchange of
pleasantries and gestures of warmth and friendliness
that made the workday something not to dread but to
look forward to. When he awoke from a night's rest,
he felt invigorated and refreshed. The air was crisp
and clean, the sun and sky clear, and like most other
inhabitants of the town, Donald soon found himself
walking the short distance to work and arriving in
good spirits. The unaccustomed exercise brought a
sparkle to his eye and a spring to his step. He looked
and felt healthier than he had for years.

As a newcomer in town Donald was invited for
dinner to the home of one of the men he worked with.
Since it turned out that both he and his host enjoyed

fishing, a fishing trip was planned for the coming weekend.

It was easy to become established in the new community. Small towns, unlike large cities, place greater value upon the individual. Soon Donald found his own impersonal habits slipping away. He began to show an interest in the people around him and in the affairs of the town. He would stop to help a youngster who had fallen from his bike and in this way come to know the child's parents. As he broadened the scope of his acquaintances, he realized he had an unsuspected capacity for making friends. This gave him a big boost in self-esteem. There was no question that he had made a wise choice when he turned his back on the kind of life that had been his in the city. He found in Colorado an environment more compatible with his personality and physical needs. He felt himself to be a different person emotionally with an abundance of energy to share with others and a heart open to receive.

Did Donald exaggerate the difficulties of city life? No, those difficulties are very evident to both the unhappy city dwellers and to the sociologists and psychologists who are studying life in large urban areas. Overpopulation, noise, and other forms of pollution have combined to take a ghastly toll of individuals who are literally locked in walls of steel and concrete.

As the 1970 census shows, nearly three quarters of the United States population now lives in large urban areas. In 1960 the urban population was 69.9 percent, but by 1970 that percentage had risen to 73.5. This also means a rise in tension for some 149,300,000 people. Even those persons who enjoy big-city life find that there are emotional and psychological hazards which cannot be totally escaped.

One of the hazards, as Donald had discovered, was the noise factor. To many people the word "pollution" suggests only dirty streets and smoky air, but "pollution" also includes noise. And noise is increasing in the cities; more automobiles and more people mean more noise.

In 1971 Dr. G. J. Thiessen reported at a Toronto meeting of the Society of Automotive Engineers that there is a steady deterioration of hearing ability among young urban residents. Dr. Thiessen, who is with the National Research Council of Canada, issued a warning that this problem could become very serious in another ten years unless something is done now about noise pollution in metropolitan areas.

There is no quiet time in the city, no relief from the steady barrage of sound. This, along with other forms of pollution, contributes substantially to the early aging of city dwellers. But more important than that, it also contributes to the loneliness. The individual who cannot make himself heard above the din will find it easier to ignore another person than to try to converse on a busy sidewalk. When you have to shout to be heard, the desire for conversation dies. Incidentally, when on one occasion automobiles were banned from a certain section in New York City, the noise level dropped to fifty-eight decibels—conversational level.

Population density is another contributing factor to big-city loneliness. The mass of people living in an urban area is defeating to the individual ego. Tension, stress, and irritation are the natural by-products of being surrounded constantly by other people, being crowded in housing, and being herded like cattle along busy sidewalks and into patterns of transportation.

A laboratory study of ducks made at Michigan State University showed that to overcrowd them resulted in their death. The affected ducks placed in stress situations suffered from a disease called amyloidosis, in which their bodies built a waxy protein up to fatal proportions in their internal organs. In man the same stress conditions produce loneliness, which may be accompanied by ulcers, headaches, or other physical symptoms.

It is also, as Muriel and Donald and thousands like them can testify, an axiomatic fact that the more people concentrated in one physical area, the less attention paid to individual personalities. There simply isn't enough time, energy, or interest in the lives of others when overcrowding means just getting through each day for yourself.

Overpopulation also means a high degree of antisocial behavior and rise in crime, particularly crimes directed against the person. Therefore, there is also a corresponding rise in suspicion and unfriendliness. It is this attitude that makes people look the other

way when they see someone being attacked or mis-
treated. City life breeds not only tension but distrust,
and the natural by-product of that is loneliness.

Fear of involvement means cutting yourself off from
other people. This fear works both ways, for there
may come a time when *you* need a helping hand, a
kind word, or some form of rescue, and then you
discover how truly alone you've become!

Involvement implies concern, love, and a willingness
to be friends. These things are all antidotes to the
poison of loneliness. Yet how rare is this kind of involvement in today's cities: Persons will give time
and energy to some impersonal cause or drive, but
they show great reluctance to become involved on a
person-to-person basis. Loneliness continues to be the
one major complaint of city dwellers, but each person
adds to the atmosphere of loneliness by his own
conduct.

Donald was able to recognize what was happening
to him and his life. There was nothing unique about
his situation. Thousands upon thousands of city dwellers are in a similar dilemma and, like Donald, have
come to realize the emptiness of their workaday
lives in an inimical environment. But there are far
fewer who have Donald's courage and deliberation to
do something about their lives before it is too late.

It is true, of course, that not everyone has the freedom of responsibility and of decision that made
Donald's choice an easy one to make. This does not
mean, though, that a modification of an unrewarding

life's pattern is impossible, no matter what the hazards.

In this enormously diversified country there is nothing to compel you to remain in a big city or in any other place where your life is empty with loneliness and lack of purpose. You may have been born in a large city, but this does not mean that you must remain there. Even if your relatives live there, do you really visit them often? Suppose you do: Undoubtedly they bring nothing substantial to your life; if they did, you would not be lonely.

What steps can you take if you feel that you are living in the wrong place? Get a good atlas, and study the country. Start a reading program about the different areas of the country. You can get help in planning your reading program from your local public library, or you can go to your favorite bookshop. Once you have covered the country in your mind, select one or two favorite areas, and then concentrate on them. Investigate the opportunities that are available in some of the smaller cities. Send for some local newspapers, and study local issues, advertisements, and notices of cultural events. Most American towns and cities have chambers of commerce equipped to furnish information about job opportunities, housing accommodations, and facts concerning weather and environmental factors, culture, and recreation.

Some kind of job can usually be found without too much difficulty—not what you were trained for, perhaps, nor anything so prestigious as the one you may now hold, but adequate to provide the necessities of life for the time being. If you are unhappy as a harassed secretary, what would you lose contenting yourself as a typist in a new place offering pleasant surroundings and friendly co-workers? If you are genuinely efficient and have a lot to give to a job, you can work your way up the ladder anywhere. In fact, talents that pass unnoticed in a more competitive environment are more readily recognized where the pace is less demanding.

Part of your loneliness problem may be associated in some way with your work or choice of occupation. Anything that contributes to your feeling of alienation also contributes to your loneliness. If your work makes you feel isolated from people, your loneliness will be correspondingly intensified.

Jim had a job on the assembly line of a large truck-manufacturing plant. He received good pay, working conditions were satisfactory, and there were many fringe benefits, yet Jim's job increased his feeling of loneliness.

"On the line," Jim explained, "I get so I feel like I'm surrounded by only machines. My mind keeps thinking, but it's like it's trapped somewhere inside my body. I feel lonely, like the only human left in a noisy, impersonal world. Some days I feel like screaming."

Despite the money and other benefits, Jim decided to look for other work. His loneliness and the stress which had built up to a dangerous level disappeared when he went to work in a small machine shop.

"Sure, I get a lot less money, and there's not the big pension program as at the X company," Jim admitted, "but here at the Y company I feel like a real person again. And this is a small enough company that they encourage you to be an individual."

Another man said he had left a large concern because there he knew that he was just a number and he wanted to be a "named" person. "All our official records were coded to social-security numbers, and this was the only way the personnel and payroll department had of identifying you," he said. "I know that this was the only efficient way to run such a large business, but it bothered me. Work was making me feel lonely and cut off from other people. I decided that the only thing I could do was to go to work for some small company where *who* you were was as important as what you did."

Like Jim, he had stopped feeling lonely when he got a job in a smaller place. If your work is making you lonely, then perhaps you need to think of making a job change.

The wrong choice of career or occupation can also add to your loneliness. One man I knew who suffered from loneliness was very unhappy in his accounting work. Unhappiness with his occupation carried over into his social life and his family life; he had difficulty in relating to other people. His work-associated dissatisfaction became a general bitterness which was directed at other people. This bitterness built a barrier between him and others. It was no wonder that he complained of being lonely! When he had the courage to change occupations and go to work in a greenhouse, he became a new person. His frustration and bitterness left him. He had a new enthusiastic personality, one that attracted other people, one that his family could enjoy. Loneliness was no longer the symptom of his unhappiness.

Take a second look at your career choice, and see if it is having some effect upon your loneliness problem. Would changing careers change the degree of loneliness in your life? Would another kind of work mean the elimination of loneliness from your life? These are all questions you will have to ask yourself —and answer.

So why not make a businesslike assessment of your situation? It is never advisable to turn one's back upon what is familiar and offers some kind of practical security without first analyzing the existing conditions (as Donald did) and evaluating the alternatives.

Begin by itemizing expenses connected with living in a crowded urban area: cleaning bills caused by the sooty air, transportation costs, high taxes and insurance, and unnecessary medical expense because crowding people together encourages the spread of infection—debilitating colds and other contagious maladies. This does not count dozens of lesser expenses you are not even aware of. How great a part of your high earnings is swallowed up by tips and gratuities and other expenses of this kind that do nothing to enrich your life or bring you, or your family, either happines or pleasure?

Can an individual who has suffered from loneliness while living in a large city find the desired measure of personal fulfillment by moving to a smaller, less populated city? Yes, if he is willing to make an effort to be friendly, to suspend some of his city attitudes of mistrust and suspicion. The person who genuinely desires to communicate with others in a warm, loving, and responsive way will have no problems in his new environment, for it is an environment that will be conducive to the type of living he needs and wants.

If you move to that smaller city, you will have to be willing to do more than change your geographical location. You will have to assume the unfamiliar habits of going out of your way to be friendly and pleasant to strangers. You will have to be willing to lower the drawbridge so that people can cross over to you. Soon you will find that the strangers have become friends, and the loneliness you felt will be like a bad dream remembered.

This is not to say that moving to another locality, out of the big city into a less crowded area, will automatically solve all your problems. These you still have to battle within yourself; that inner put-down force that wishes you to be lonely must be overcome. You will have far more equipment to wage battle with, though, and more energy for self-improvement, since you won't be dissipating it in trying to fight off noise and foul odors, rush and overcrowding.

When was the last time you walked down a quiet, shady street in the springtime, with the sunshine filtering through the treetops and the smell of lilacs all around? When did you last have the quiet in which to meditate, to empty your mind of the trivia and distractions that oppress your spirit?

Life is short and often uncertain, but you do have some choice as to how you will live it. Shouldn't you try to find a place of beauty, free of environmental annoyances, where you have time and opportunity to know people and to achieve your heartfelt desires?

Not everyone can escape the turmoil and pressures of the big city, nor does everyone wish to. There are those whose temperament is attuned to the fast pace, the excitement, and the chaotic activity that only big-city life can offer. But for those who are unable to survive the environmental crush and have no tolerance for the accelerated tempo—for those who find the omnipresent ego impingements physically and emotionally destructive—a strong case can be made for the advantages of turning one's back on whatever material advantages may appear to exist and striking out for some other region and a simpler pattern of life.

If this is *not* possible, there are positive programs to be pursued while living in a big city in which it is possible to solve the problem of loneliness. First of all, the environmental impact and its debilitating influence can be greatly lessened if one takes advantage of every opportunity—weekends, vacations, holidays—to get out into the country or otherwise shift into a different setting. We all need change in our lives to refresh our sensitivities and expand our perspectives. We still have unspoiled countryside, parks, and even wilderness areas that man's proneness to devastate has not yet destroyed. While they are still ours to enjoy, we should take advantage of this national heritage which, in a real way, is our own property.

Since much of the alienation felt in cities results from the breakdown of family and neighborhood, this, too, can be alleviated. Don't be a loner. Create a family of your own. We all need a sense of belonging. Some of us get it from an exceptional job situation, but this is rarely enough. Often a substitute family is closer in spirit and compatibility than the family into which one may have been born.

It is this search for a substitute family that accounts for the popularity of communes. Urban communal living is not a back-to-the-land movement; it is an attempt to find familial closeness with responsible and responsive people. There are many such well-established and flourishing communes which are specifically designed to appeal to middle-class, professional, and older citizens. Communes include both married couples and single people.

Members of a White House panel on family structure in the United States conducted a survey in 1970 and found many positive aspects about the adult communes. They recognized that these communes are one way in which some persons fight their daily battle of loneliness.

How successful are these communes? As with any living situation the success or failure depends upon the individual. A commune member has to be willing to pay his share, do his share, and accept group discipline. Most persons admit that they joined in communal-living arrangements because they were unhappy living alone. As one member, an architect, said in a newspaper interview, "I was lonely. . . ." This problem of personal loneliness probably accounts for the popularity of the estimated more than three thousand communes in this country. Incidentally, two-thirds of those communes are located in urban areas.

Communal living, which is really a form of family extension, suits only a small minority of people. For them it is the solution, but for others adult communal living still means living with strangers and is not a satisfactory surrogate for the family. These people need to look for other ways of satisfying their desire for family life and love. Loneliness for them persists because they miss their own family, from which they may be removed because of geographic or psychological reasons.

If love for your own family is missing, you should not feel guilty. A friend of mine, a famous bishop, once told me that the biblical admonition to honor one's father and mother applied only if one's parents successfully fulfill their parental roles. Parental failure is often at fault, for the loneliness that pursues you in later life is caused by their having set the stage originally. If your personal family has never satisfied your emotional needs, perhaps you will find this satisfaction in a close association with some other person —a neighbor, a co-worker, a fellow commuter. Blood kinship is not a requirement for qualities of warmth and understanding, so if these are wanting in your relationship with the members of your original family, this does not mean they cannot be found elsewhere.

Rather than dwell upon the dissatisfying relationship you have had in the past with your own family, look around you, and see if you can't find one more to your liking. There are ready-made families replete with mother and father, brothers and sisters, eager to welcome some outside individual who can bring color and diversity to *their* lives by contributing something of himself.

How does one go about acquiring such a family? You may yourself initiate an opportunity by organizing a rotating dinner club among your acquaintances in which each member provides one course; or depending upon your personal interests, there are music and reading clubs that afford opportunity for meeting people and seeking out mutual likes and dislikes which result in compatible relationships. But it is necessary—compulsory, in fact—that you yourself contribute something. You must give of yourself in some degree, whether it is an act of consideration or kindness, an interested query, or a clever anecdote. If you hope to be "adopted" into an intimate family circle, you must have a willingness to give as well as the capacity to receive. These are basic credentials of good fellowship desired no less in a family situation than if you are a candidate for membership in a select social club or fraternity.

It is good to remember that small families are the closest. Don't take a "love-me-love-my-dog" tack with these people, who have taken you into the warmth of their family group, by expecting them also to take in all the other loners and social misfits of your acquaintance. You are seeking the warmth and shelter, the give and take, the love and understanding, of a family; this is not the same as organizing a social club.

In any case the secret to overcoming loneliness is to develop your sensitivities from the inside out. Even though you belong to the human race, you are first of all an individual, differing in most particulars from every other person on this earth. This is your greatest human attribute. You should, therefore, heed the bidding of your private self, your interior being. It will make your self so much better and elevate your self-esteem.

The Lonely Child

It is easy to forget childhood loneliness. That is, it is easy to forget it if you have become a well-adjusted adult. It is easy to ignore childhood loneliness if you are a busy adult. It is very easy to dismiss the whole idea of childhood loneliness if you prefer to keep to the conclusion that children have no emotional ups and downs, no problems. The truth is that they do, and we as parents, teachers, or simply as adults can contribute unthinkingly and unwittingly to childhood loneliness. In many other instances we fail to recognize the causes and symptoms of this loneliness.

What makes a child lonely? And what can you, as a concerned adult, do to alleviate the situation? These are some of the questions we will try to answer in this chapter.

One of the common causes of childhood loneliness is the feeling of being unloved and unwanted. It is true that this may often be the result of misunderstanding or misinterpretation on the part of the child. He does not always understand the adult world and adult interests. Children are self-centered. It is only as they grow in emotional maturity that they are able to accept the fact that they cannot always be the center of attention. During childhood, when they are so emotionally and physically dependent upon their parents and other adults, it is difficult for them to accept the fact that adults have other interests and areas of life which do not include them.

It is socially and psychologically proper that children be excluded from certain adult activities. A child is therefore by necessity excluded from adult entertainments and other social activities, adult love and sex life, and adult intellectual pursuits.

For example, Barry, who was six, became emotionally upset whenever his parents went out to a restaurant or to some other evening entertainment without him. When questioned, Barry readily admitted that he felt "left out" and "bad" when he was not allowed to accompany his parents. He cried because he did not like being excluded from the things his parents did.

Part of Barry's loneliness problem was based on a misinterpretation of what adult life is, and part of it could be attributed to his mother. Barry had been a sickly baby, and his mother still worried about his health. She kept a close and watchful eye on him when he was home. She did not encourage him to play with other children. After being made to feel very important all day long, Barry was upset when he felt that he was put aside for adult activities.

Barry's whole world was his home, his family, and, in particular, his mother. He did not comprehend emotionally that his parents could have other interests in their lives besides those of home and Barry.

Through counseling Barry was able to understand more about the adult world and to accept the differences between adult interests and his own. At the same time Barry's mother had to change her attitude. She had to encourage Barry to develop a work-play relationship with other children. Naturally when she was the focal point of his life, he was going to feel lonely when she appeared to be deserting him for other people and other things.

Incidentally, whereas older children will say that they feel "lonely," the concept of loneliness does not always have meaning for younger children. They may say they feel "bad," as Barry said, or they may complain of some physical symptom. It is usually a stomachache or some symptom related to the gastrointestinal system. This is an unconscious choice but a very natural one from a psychological point of view. Children are primarily oral characters at this point. Nourishment is not only important and necessary to them, but food has emotional meaning in their lives. They associate food and eating with their mothers. When they feel lonely or disappointed in their parents, the first reaction is one related to oral dependency.

Loneliness for a person of any age is a situation threatening the personality. To the lonely child there is added the ingredient of personal immaturity which makes adjustment difficult without understanding and help.

When your child or a child you know says, "My stomach hurts," listen carefully, for he may really be saying, "I'm lonely."

The child who feels left out of family life may express his loneliness and unhappiness in patterns of disobedience and other forms of misbehavior. Again, this behavior is hiding the basic problem—loneliness. Parents frequently refuse to accept the fact that their child is lonely. They feel that this is a reflection upon their capabilities as parents. They feel that to be told their child is lonely is something either shameful or untrue.

This was the case with Steve's parents, who had sought help for their eight-year-old son. The boy had become a problem because of his behavior. Both parents expressed indignation when told that he was lonely and that his malicious behavior at home and in school was his way of showing his loneliness.

"Do you mean to tell me that that kid hacked at

my golf clubs because he was lonely?" snorted the father.

"Steve can't be lonely," protested the mother. "We give him everything. He goes to the best school. He has all kinds of toys, a lovely room of his own. We never leave him alone. We always make sure that the maid is there when we are gone."

They did give Steve all of the material things that a child could need or want. They did not consider his emotional needs, though—only his physical ones. They did not give anything very personal of themselves to their child. In Steve's mind the maid, although a kind woman, was not the right substitute for his mother, whom he loved and missed. There was also a conscious message on his part when he tried to destroy his father's golf clubs. He was expressing his loneliness at being left alone while his father played golf.

Like adults, children become resentful and angry when they are lonely. Unlike adults, children do not try to cover up these angry feelings; they express them openly, directly, and sometimes forcefully. But when Steve was characterized by his father as "spiteful," he should have been called "lonely."

Steve's parents were able to face the fact of their own parental neglect and his subsequent loneliness. They were willing, once this point had been reached, to try to change the structure of their family life so that Steve would have some share in their activities. They were able to give him a strong sense of family unity and parental love and concern. As soon as Steve felt that he was an important part of his family, his malicious behavior ceased.

Anxiety can cause childhood loneliness. This anxiety is often based on half-truths or overheard and misunderstood conversations. One child, hearing his parents quarrel over money, misinterpreted his father's remark, "You are ruining us," to mean that his parents would be separating. He immediately felt lonely and upset when he thought the security of his family world was threatened.

Any change, or sometimes even the suggestion of change, can have an adverse emotional effect upon children. Loneliness goes along with a move to a new neighborhood or a new school or even the vague possibility of such a move. Loneliness results when there is a change in the family circle. Loneliness comes about whenever there are stress situations.

"I never dreamed that my little girl would feel lonely because of her grandmother's illness. In fact, I tried to hide it from her. I thought she was too young to understand or to be worried by such unpleasantness," one mother told me.

What she had not realized was that her daughter would be aware of her mother's anxiety and preoccupation. In addition, the child felt lonely because she was not altogether sure of what was happening to her grandmother. There was the unresolved loneliness caused by a very natural fear of the ultimate in change—death.

Children are more emotionally resilient than parents like to believe, and they can have a surprising grasp of difficult and painful situations. It is not helpful to try to protect them by shutting them out of family crises, for what they do not know, they will imagine. Telling your child the truth in terms that he can easily comprehend will keep loneliness from developing during times of family tension.

Too often we forget just how dependent children are upon adults. They have to look to adults for survival. No one ever condones or accepts the premise of child abuse, and yet many adults are guilty of mistreating children in an emotional sense.

It is possible for a parent to make a child feel unloved and unwanted. That child, feeling rejected by his parents, will have so little self-esteem that he is unable to get along well with others outside of the family circle. He becomes the loner who refuses to take part in group play. He does not know how to mix with his peer group. He becomes suspicious of overtures made by other adults, since they may prove to be as unreliable and eventually as unloving as his parents. He is a lonely misfit at an early age, often using defiance and indifference as a disguise to hide his loneliness.

There are many events that occur naturally in the adult world that can bring about loneliness in children, unless, of course, those events are properly explained. The birth of a baby brother or sister is one of the most common causes of childhood loneliness. This new child is a threat to the older one. Loneliness sets in as the parents, particularly the mother, and other adults become preoccupied with the baby. But similar feelings of rejection and loneliness can occur when the parents take in a new friend or a new interest.

Mike's parents developed an interest in art after meeting a couple who were professional artists. Soon the new couple were made part of the family circle. There was nothing wrong with that except that Mike was shunted aside as his parents talked and planned with the new people. Mike felt that he was no longer of interest to them, since he was unable to take part in the art discussions. When his parents began to do artwork themselves, they seemed to have even less time for him. A climax was reached when Mike was discovered trying to destroy one of his mother's paintings.

At first Mike's parents were angry with him, then they tried to understand what had brought him to this point of desperation. Mike himself was frightened by what he had tried to do, and while sobbing, he finally admitted that he was lonesome. Fortunately his parents were able to put themselves in his place.

"I guess I would have been lonely and angry, too," Mike's father said. "After all, suddenly we did not appear interested in him anymore."

The problem was solved by letting Mike share their interest in art. The new friends were made part of the plan, and they included Mike in some of their discussions. Mike was given his own set of paints, and he was encouraged to make his own pictures. Since Mike no longer felt threatened by the new people or his parents' interest in art, he got over his loneliness. He became content to play while his parents pursued their hobby. He understood that they did not love him less because they had friends and things to do.

Children are very willing to let adults alone, but they do want the assurance that they are not totally forgotten during those periods.

Parents who are gregarious by nature must be sure that their children do not feel left out while they entertain other adults. This is not to say that children are to be a part of adult social life, but rather that they should not feel that they are unwanted by their parents. In a good parent-child relationship both sides know that there are times that belong solely to the one group. A child in such a relationship will know his parents' friends but will not expect to be included in all adult social activities.

The very physical surroundings of a child can produce feelings of isolation and loneliness. Try looking at the world through the eyes of a child. A child is literally dwarfed by buildings, the landscape, furniture, and other objects. His world is filled with large machines (automobiles) and rushing giants (adults). Even a child who never gets lost in the actual sense of the word may have periods in which he feels lost. This sense of being lost means being lonely.

A child must learn to cope with the adult world with its many learning situations. To a large extent he is a very small wanderer in a very big world. It is far too easy to make a child feel like a stranger in the adult-centered world. Wouldn't you feel lonely in such a world?

This is why it is important to set aside special times and occasions for sharing with children. You as adults must build a bridge between childhood and adulthood so that there are times of mutual sharing of interests.

Since children must be excluded from that special love shared by husband and wife, it is important to give them a feeling of the special and unique love between parent and child.

In one family the father made it a point to take his children out individually for special outings and recreational events. No one felt lonely when another child had his or her turn or when the parents went out. Each child knew that he enjoyed his special measure of his father's love. A mother, too, should make it a point to have a special area of sharing and love with her children so that they do not feel lonely when she shares something special with her husband.

It should be understood in a family that each person, adult or child, is an individual and has worth and importance as an individual. The child who feels loved does not resent the time his parents spend with each other or the affection they show each other.

You can help eliminate feelings of loneliness in your child by spending part of family recreational time doing things that include the child. Naturally there are occasions that are suitable only for adults, but you can plan others to include your child. For example, you and your spouse may enjoy going to plays or adult-oriented movies, but you should also arrange your time so that you can enjoy the zoo with your child or go to a matinee of a family movie. You can read books aloud. You can read the funnies together on a Sunday morning. Yes, these do take time, but they go a long way toward removing childhood loneliness.

Fear can make a child lonely. This is especially true in cases where the child does not have an adult in whom he can confide. Fear is an isolating emotion. Fear is a breeding ground for loneliness, especially in children. Adults can often rationalize their fears or turn to others for help, but children do not always have that ability or confidence in others.

The fear of failure can be so overwhelming to a child that it keeps him apart from others. It makes him a lonely child. Parents may unconsciously encourage this state to develop by their demands upon a child. The child reasons that failure will mean displeasure and then estrangement from his parents. This produces anxiety, which in turn produces a state of loneliness.

Here is the way one small boy, Dick, aged nine, described the situation: "I'm not good at games, but my father keeps wanting me to be. I try, but the other guys are all better. He insisted that I play baseball this summer. When he comes to watch the games,

I make all kinds of mistakes that I didn't make during practice. I feel funny and afraid when I look up and see him sitting there watching me. I know he wishes that Billy, our star pitcher, was his boy instead of me. When we go home, he doesn't say anything. I guess I'm just about the most miserable kid I know."

In this case we could translate the word "miserable" as used by Dick to mean "lonely." Dick had the fear of failing at baseball plus the fear of displeasing his father. He knew that his inability to please his father in baseball was resulting in alienation from him. Of course, Dick could not have put all of his feelings of loneliness into such succinct terms, but he suffered from the effects of that loneliness.

As parents we should always consider whether or not we are being realistic in terms of the child's actual ability when we make achievement demands on him. Too often a parent tries to relive his or her own life in terms of his child, insisting that the child succeed in a specific sport or field of study.

Children want to please those whom they love. They are very much aware of their parents' approval or disapproval. Knowing that they have failed or fearing that they *might* fail makes the child feel tense and alone.

We have already spoken about the loneliness that happens to a child when a new baby comes into the family, but there is always the potential for loneliness to develop because of sibling differences.

A child who is younger may feel lonely because he

sees his older brother or sister having certain privileges and certain relationships with adult family members from which he is excluded due to his age. An older child may feel lonely and resentful if he feels that the younger children in the family are too much the center of parental attention.

It is part of being a good parent to see that each child understands his place within the family circle and feels secure in it. The thirteen-year-old will know that he has certain privileges and responsibilities that his five-year-old sibling does not have. He should understand that in a very real sense he has exchanged his earlier dependence and babyish ways for these new attitudes which are closer to the adult world. Your five-year-old can be taught that he has certain needs which are different from those of his older sisters and brothers and that those needs are going to be met.

Any form of favoritism in the family group will mean that someone else is going to feel left out and lonely. The age of the shut-out child doesn't matter; what *does* matter is his sense of loneliness.

Each child in the family should know that he is getting the concern and attention that is appropriate to his development and age. The younger child will have more direct care from the parents in terms of his feeding, body cleanliness, and physical needs. The older child will have more contact with his parents in the areas of ideas and intellectual communication. Basic to all age groups, however, is the need to be loved and understood. This is the best preventive of loneliness.

Children feel lonely when they are put into a social situation that is unfamiliar to them. Because they have had limited contacts and experiences in inter-personal relations, they are not sure of how they should react to new people or new things.

A child faced with a totally new situation may feel that it is *he* who is different. He feels alone because he doesn't know what to do. It seems to him that every-one else knows just what to do or say. A child wants to do the correct thing. He doesn't like to be laughed at because he has done the wrong thing.

Try watching a group of children gathered for a party, and you can easily spot the child or children who feel uneasy and lonely. They are the ones who stay to one side, by themselves. Their posture sug-gests stiffness from fright and loneliness.

Parents do try to prepare their children emotionally for certain group and social situations such as the start of school, going to the dentist or the doctor for the first time, and similar events. Too many parents stop there with what we might call stock situations. They mistakenly feel that if their child gets along well at home or in his neighborhood, he is automatically going to feel at home in a social situation involving strangers and new situations. This is not true. A child is not born with poise; he learns it, and he needs the understanding help of the adults in his life.

You can keep your child from being one of the

lonely ones by taking time to discuss upcoming new situations with him. Help him to be prepared emotionally and socially when he meets strangers or is placed in an unfamiliar setting. Give your child the assurance of feeling adequate.

It is a popular misconception that children do not become suicidal because of loneliness and other emotional problems. The truth is that many people, especially parents, are unwilling to accept this as a fact. Until the nineteenth century there were no statistics available on childhood suicide, although there were the same kinds of childhood problems as now. However, as more attention was paid to children as individuals, more statistical concern was also shown. The results shocked many people. In recent years there has been an increase in suicides among young people. In a report issued by the National Clearinghouse for Mental Health Information, "Suicide among Youth," we find the results of various studies and statistics. The danger period for youthful suicides as shown in these figures is the ages just preceding adolescence. (Adolescent suicide figures will be discussed in Chapter 8.) What we are talking about is primarily the years between eight and fourteen.

One of the problems with getting reliable statistics for childhood suicides is that often such a death is not so reported. As stated in "Suicide among Youth":

Possibly suicides of the young are even more shameful and embarrassing to survivors than are adult suicides. Accordingly there may be a greater concealment of suicide at younger ages. Moreover, youngsters may be less likely to leave notes for bona-fide evidence and adults may be more likely to dismiss the prospect of suicidal intent in children than in older children.

Adults feel accused when a child commits suicide. They prefer to believe that it was an "accident" rather than a crying out against life.

Counselors and investigators have found that children commit or consider suicide for reasons that have to do with family problems, feelings of failure, lack of self-esteem, and loneliness. Children do have a tendency to overreact to their feelings and especially to their feelings of insecurity. In fact, some researchers have indicated that there is reason to suppose that young children who commit suicide do not really understand the permanence of death.

The lonely child may be the child in your classroom; he or she may be the child next door, or the child in your own family. No matter what your adult problems and concerns are, you have the responsibility to be aware of the child and his problems. The best prescription for childhood loneliness is this awareness on the part of adults. Understanding children should mean *loving* them, and the child who feels loved does not feel lonely.

8

The Lonely Adolescent

There is universal agreement that the period of adolescence is a difficult one. It is difficult in terms of the many physical and emotional changes that take place. This age has always been a favorite of writers, because within the adolescent years is encompassed a microcosm of all the emotions that affect individuals. From the beginning there has been a fascination with this particular age group because of the very naked quality of the emotional upheaval experienced during this period. From such books as Johann von Goethe's *The Sorrows of Young Werther* and Booth Tarkington's *Seventeen* to the works of J. D. Salinger there have been attempts to portray the "storm and stress" of these important formative years.

Adolescence is a time of dramatic individual change. As with any bodily or mental state its onset and duration may vary according to the individual, but in general we say that adolescence, or puberty, is coincidental with the teen years. The age of adolescence, because of its inherent inner turmoil, forces loneliness onto the growing youth. Adolescence as a time of personality development and self-discovery can easily lead to periods of intense situational loneliness when the young boy or girl comes to the conclusion that "nobody understands me!"

This loneliness and sense of isolation during adolescence can also have positive aspects despite the basic feelings of unhappiness. Since, as I have said, adolescence is a period when the teen-ager discovers himself as a person, these lonely times are times of self-analysis, which can lead to better self-knowledge. Adolescent loneliness can also be the period during which the young individual works out in his mind his relationships with others and the world in general. It does not need to be a lonely time of standing still in life, but a time during which slow but steady steps toward maturity are taken.

Another positive aspect of adolescent loneliness is that it can lead the adolescent to develop his creative abilities. It is during this time that he can experiment with activities and hobbies until he finds the one that most satisfies his needs. In the meantime he has also solved the situational loneliness problem for himself.

Too often, parents and other adults make the mistake of trying to help adolescents over this natural time of temporary loneliness by forcing them into social or other activities. Normal adolescence means time alone; it means *some* temporary loneliness, but this very idea seems to terrify most parents. They often give the impression that if they have a lonely child, it is a reflection on themselves as parents. The wise parent recognizes that loneliness not only is a part of growing up but will have to be solved by the young person himself. The adolescent who never comes to grips with his loneliness will not be able to cope with problems of loneliness when he becomes an adult. Most of the cases I have seen of adults who were suffering from emotional problems related to loneliness also had histories of being unable to handle loneliness when they were adolescents.

Here are the ways in which two families met this question of adolescent loneliness and handled it, one with success and one with failure. Both families had teen-age boys who were going through normal emotional growth periods in which there were times of withdrawal and loneliness. The C. family recognized this and let their boy develop toward maturity by not forcing themselves or their activities on him. They did try to help him by providing seemingly casual activities in which he could join and feel a part of the group. They also gave him a camera when he expressed a rather vague longing to "do something worthwhile" with his time. Soon he was not concerned with his temporary loneliness, because he was too busy taking pictures. From taking pictures it was a natural step to want to take a photography class and later to join a camera club. By the time he had reached that step he was able to use his time alone in a constructive way and at other times be with people on a social level. His loneliness period had been a period in which the C. boy had developed his own personality.

In contrast to this the D. family could not let their boy alone. They were vocally sympathetic with his being lonely and insisted on making him engage in various social activities in which he was neither interested nor capable. As a result his loneliness became more pronounced, even though he was constantly surrounded by other people. When he was alone, he became easily depressed and at a loss as to what to do. By the end of adolescence the boy was completely dependent upon others for his emotional peace of mind. He had never progressed toward maturity but instead had regressed to an infantile level in terms of his emotional development.

Interestingly enough, whereas most people try to ignore the problems of childhood loneliness, nearly everyone is willing to concede that loneliness frequently accompanies adolescence. An adult who can remember his or her own adolescence in accurate and realistic terms will usually admit that there were periods of depression and loneliness.

Frequently these periods are extreme and at the time seem to be overwhelming. Fortunately adolescence is transitional. Emotions do simmer down, or rather, limits of control are developed by the young person as he reaches out toward adult maturity.

To some parents and to many adolescents it may seem as if this difficult period will never end! Patience is limited in the young, and this is why some adolescents are unable to cope with their problems of loneliness, tension, and depression. They therefore need understanding and concern from adults who are associated with them.

Desperation and the typical dramatic flair of that age level lead many adolescents to seek a solution of their problems in death. It has been estimated that in the United States about one thousand boys and girls between the ages of fourteen and twenty-one commit suicide each year. There are no doubt thousands of others who try and fail and many more who entertain some notion of suicide at various times.

Unlike children, adolescents are aware of what death is and how final it is. And although some suicides are drug-induced or based on impulsive acts, most youthful suicides or attempted suicides have a history of unhappiness, fears, or loneliness behind them. Those who look to suicide as a solution already feel alone in this world, so they are able to rationalize their way out of it into the unknown.

Adolescents do not have enough experience in living —experience that makes it possible to tolerate a high degree of disappointment and failure. Adults have had to learn this toleration in order to survive in life.

Adolescents, however, are less likely to compromise with loneliness and other emotional problems.

In addition to the unmistakable forms of suicide that occur, there is a high accident level for the adolescent age group, particularly accidents involving automobiles and motorcycles. It is thought that many of these so-called accidents are not accidents at all but deliberate attempts at self-destruction. The recklessness of youth is only partly attributable to a lack of judgment; some of it is based on a contempt for life and a desire for death.

What causes these adolescent traumas? What causes loneliness to develop in young people? Loneliness is undoubtedly the plague of those teen years. It is, in fact, a built-in risk as young people grow and begin to become individuals.

In discovering himself and building a strong sense of personal identity, the adolescent is forced to separate himself from his childhood dependency patterns. It is a time of rebellion. Frequently parents and children find to their amazement that they are suddenly on opposite sides. It is then that we hear such comments as these: "My folks don't understand me anymore"; "My daughter used to tell me everything, but now I never know what she's thinking or doing"; "My mother is too old-fashioned—she doesn't realize times have changed"; and "My son used to look up to me, but now he acts as though I don't have any sense!"

There is indignation, bewilderment, and resentment

on both sides. The result is a temporary split in family unity, an alienation that leads to adolescent loneliness.

One reason why the young person feels lonely is that he feels disloyalty in questioning his parents and their standards, yet this rebellion is a natural part of growing up and achieving maturity. Rebellion is one way in which the individual establishes a sense of personal autonomy and identity. This is necessary so that eventually the young person can leave his parents and his childhood home and establish his own life and home.

It *does* produce loneliness—this breakaway process —and it is a part of normal adolescence. The adolescent no longer sees his parents as the absolute rulers of his private world. He now sees their faults, he disagrees with them and their generation, and he wants to put forth his own ideas and have them accepted. But he is not far enough removed from childhood that he can totally lose his emotional dependence upon his parents. He feels and is lonely at times because he misses the close relationship he had with his parents. Unconsciously he misses the uncomplicated, unquestioning warmth and dependence they shared as a family when he was a child.

As one adolescent girl put it, "Sometimes I feel so sad and lonely. It seems as if I am on a boat drifting away, and my parents are on the shore. I want to be with them, but I also want to get away."

Parents and adults who are associated with adolescents are often shocked by the violence of the instinctual upheaval that is a part of the adolescent years. They sometimes find it hard to understand why the young people have to go through such dramatic changes.

"My son is so moody now that he is a teen-ager," one mother complained. "He used to be such a happy little boy that I feel like he's a completely different person."

He *was* a different person from the child his mother had known. He could not understand why she was surprised at the way he felt. After all, he had changed physically and no longer looked like her "little boy," and there were corresponding emotional and mental changes as well. Naturally he felt moody and lonely because his mother was not able to accept him as a new person. He felt isolated from her. He saw himself as becoming a man; she still saw him as a child.

Another mother complained that her adolescent daughter would no longer take part in family affairs and social activities. "Mary is so emotional! She cries and says that she is lonely, but she refuses to do things with us anymore. Last week we all went to the state fair, but she wouldn't go with us. She said she'd rather stay home and feel lonely! I don't understand her. I don't know what to do with her, and yet sometimes she can be so helpful, and she even seems interested in family things."

It was difficult for this mother to see her daughter trying to cut the family ties so that she could grow up as a person. There was a seesaw reaction as Mary would try to be independent and then would go back to her former place of dependency in the family circle. She vacillated between childhood and young adulthood. She was lonely because she felt the necessity of cutting herself off, of separating herself from her family, and yet she felt guilty and unhappy at doing this.

What can you as a concerned parent or other adult do to help during this period? For one thing you will have to be willing to accept these off-and-on-again relationships without feeling personally hurt and offended. You will have to realize that on Monday you may be taken into your adolescent's confidence, but on Tuesday you may be rebuffed. Nothing will be gained on either side if you attempt to force him to regress to the childhood dependency state. You will have to be willing to meet him on his new level of development. You will have to be willing to engage in a meaningful dialogue with him. You have to be willing to let him argue and shout if necessary without losing your temper. Adolescence is a learning time, but it is not one of automatic respect and docility.

Mutual tolerance and a realistic attitude toward adolescence will do much to lessen the tension between generations. It will also help to alleviate adolescent loneliness. You do not have to agree with the adolescent's ideas to make him feel that he has something to say. If you are just willing to give him some time and attention, he will feel an appreciation and love that takes away that sense of isolation and loneliness.

An adolescent feels lonely when he feels the need to establish a personal identity which is different from that of his parents. At no other time in our cultural history was there such a generation gap as now. The Vietnam war, the problems of pollution and overpopulation, as well as differing attitudes on drugs, civil disobedience, and sexual standards have successfully divided adolescents from adults.

There is a special loneliness that comes to an adolescent when he believes that his parents do not maintain the standards of altruistic conduct that he thought they did. There is a special loneliness that develops when the adolescent realizes that his parents are not going to change their pattern of living and philosophical concepts. It takes time, possibly a few years, before the two generations can come together again comfortably on certain moral and political issues. Until that time the adolescent feels let down by his parents.

It is not easy for parents to listen while their faults are listed and catalogued by angry and disappointed offspring, yet more is to be gained by listening than by shouting back.

"Having no one to talk to!" is a common complaint of adolescents. What they mean is that they have no adult who is willing to listen to them. Adolescents talk to each other, but they want to talk to people who have had more life experience than their own. They want to learn by sharing thoughts and ideas. Loneliness sets in when they are unable to establish patterns of meaningful dialogue with adults.

Anxiety about the future can cause adolescent loneliness. Parents frequently do not understand this anxiety. As one father said, "Why should my kids be worried? I provide for them. They will go to college. They have what they need."

But his son when asked, said, "I worry because I'm not sure whether or not I should go to college. Besides there's the war. I don't know what my folks would say if I said I would not go and fight. I'd like to be able to discuss various alternatives with my father, but he sees life in only one way and he sees *my* life in only one way."

The two adolescent daughters in this family also reported that they were not so sure of what they wanted to do as their father seemed to be for them. All three children reported varying degrees of loneliness and isolation feelings. They felt regret at this lack of communication between themselves and their father. They wanted to be able to talk over their hopes, fears, and problems without being told they had nothing to worry about.

Chronic loneliness can develop during adolescence as the instinctual upheavals of this period tend to isolate the individual. Sexual drives and aggressive impulses are sometimes so little understood by the adolescent that he turns away from others, especially parents and other adult authority figures. To put it plainly, they are scared by these new feelings that threaten to overwhelm them. A boy or girl may think that his or her sexual impulses or aggressive drives are unique and strange. Trying to hide these natural feelings can easily lead to a pattern of estrangement from others. It means not only emotional suffering for the adolescent, but loneliness, too.

The boy whose father has forbidden him to take the car may have a fantasy in which he not only takes the car in defiance of that order but injures or kills the father to do so. Such a daydream may seriously upset the boy. He feels guilty and unworthy and avoids his father.

All adolescents have times at which they act out their rebellious feelings in such fantasies. These are escape valves for their highly emotional and volatile feelings. In addition, all adolescents have sexual fantasies which may include acts of violence. If the adolescent is made to feel ashamed of such fantasies, or if he fears them, he may withdraw completely and become immersed in loneliness.

The wise and loving parent tries to bridge this gap and to make the adolescent understand that he is, in a sense, trying on various disguises and acting out various roles during this period. The adolescent who has a welcoming adult to go to and ask about these drives and impulses is able to get over his loneliness.

The adolescent must go through a period when he feels like an outsider, but it does not have to be of long duration. It is possible for the adults in a family to so moderate their attitudes that the young person can feel independent and closely related at the same time, without ever feeling completely isolated.

A child can run to his parents and express his primary need for affection and intimacy, but an adolescent does not feel that same sense of freedom, although he has the same need. He, too, wants physical contact and companionship, but it is less easy for him to get these needs fulfilled. He does get this from his peer group, but not from adults. An adolescent may mistakenly feel that these needs are too babyish to be answered, yet he is lonely because they are not answered. The understanding adult who is with adolescents knows that there are times when physical expressions of loving concern are needed rather than words.

"I was really feeling blue and lonely one day," a sixteen-year-old girl told us. "I was trying to study, but nothing seemed to click. My teacher, Miss Smith, walked past my desk. She didn't say a thing but leaned over and patted me on the shoulder. It was just a second, but it made me feel better. I felt someone cared. I didn't feel so lonely."

The increase in mobility in modern times has contributed to adolescent loneliness. In former times families were in one place and had their roots in that place. The members of the family group tended to congregate in the same geographical area. If an adolescent had problems with parents, there was always another adult relative—an aunt, a cousin, an uncle, or a grandparent—to whom he could turn. Some of the traditional loneliness associated with growing up was dissipated by the very fact that the young person knew his family had been in one place for generations and would continue as a unity. Now, however, families scatter, and it is rare to find several generations living in close proximity. More and more adolescents have a history of being born in one town and raised in other towns. This moving about, which is usually tied to economic reasons, does mean a certain amount of loneliness for the young person who is not permitted to feel rooted to any place.

What mobility does to the sense of belonging can be counteracted by a family feeling of belonging. If parents make the child or young person feel that home in the true sense of the word is within the family circle, moving around will not have any lasting effects of depression and loneliness. Naturally there will always be some temporary loneliness during the time of adjustment to new surroundings.

Adults are sometimes disturbed by adolescent bragging and lying. Again, these are indications of loneliness. They are part of the role-playing we mentioned earlier in the chapter. An adolescent feels the need to compete not only with his peers but with adults. He may decide that he has to resort to falsehood and bragging because he feels deficient in competitive areas. This sense of personal inadequacy makes him feel lonely and sometimes angry. To compensate he verbalizes his daydreams and fantasies. This is frequently the case in sexual matters. The adolescent boy, in particular, feels compelled to brag about supposed sexual conquests or adventures. All of this is simply part of growing up. The alert adult should realize, however, that the more an adolescent brags or lies, the less sure of himself he really is. In all likelihood he is a lonely teen-ager.

The boy or girl who during adolescence lags behind his or her peers in physical development or personal achievements will become lonely. Popularity is very important to the adolescent. He wants to be liked. He wants to be one of the gang or group. Not to belong seems like a disaster to the teen-ager. His loneliness is intensified when he sees others having a good time or meeting in an easy camaraderie.

Parents can help during this period by being understanding and offering assistance in more practical ways. In one family the father offered to teach chess to a group of adolescents after noticing that his own son, who was a brilliant boy lacking in social skills, was developing the habits and personality of a loner. Soon his son had friends who respected him for his ability to play chess and similar games and could good-naturedly accept his deficiencies in other areas such as body-contact sports

Adolescents have to be taught how to give and take, and they are very willing to accept differences in personalities once they have been exposed to them.

In a society that places undue emphasis upon

beauty and good looks the plain or homely adolescent is apt to feel lonely. Parents, teachers, or other adults should be sure that emphasis is placed on personality rather than on physical attractiveness. There is a special danger trap in a family in which one child may be very pretty or handsome while another is not. Comparisons between the two will make the plain child feel lonely. He or she will feel unwanted and ugly.

"My mother was always sighing because I was not as pretty as my two older sisters," one woman told us. "I really suffered as a teen-ager. I refused to go to school dances and other teen-age activities because I just knew I was unpopular on account of my looks. I remember how unhappy and lonely I felt as I would see my sisters going off on dates. I realize now how foolish that was because I really wasn't that bad-looking. It was my family that had made me feel that way. I finally got over it and learned that there were other things besides being pretty."

Parents can give their adolescents personality security by respecting them as individuals and in cases where there are several adolescents in the same family, by being able to accept the differences between them without making unfair or odious comparisons.

Loneliness may drive a teen-ager into a hasty and unfortunate marriage. The adolescent who is looking for security and warmth may mistakenly think he can get it from marriage. He (or she) sees marriage only as a cure for loneliness without considering the other aspects of the marriage situation. Adolescent boys and girls may marry to solve their loneliness problems but find that they have complicated their lives in other basic ways—in financial areas, for instance.

An adolescent girl who feels very lonely will sometimes turn to an older man. As one woman said, "I was very lonely and insecure as an adolescent. I admired my parents and their friends because they seemed to be so sure of themselves. I despaired of ever achieving the same degree of assurance and sophistication. When an older man, a friend of my father, began to pay attention to me, I was flattered and relieved. It seemed to me that by marrying him I would automatically get over my loneliness and my lack of sophistication."

This same woman, while admitting that her marriage had worked out, nevertheless said that she was going to be more alert to the needs and emotions of her children so that loneliness would not drive them into questionable marriage situations.

Adolescent development is accompanied by a certain amount of introspection and introversion. The teenager spends much of his time looking at himself, thinking about himself, and analyzing his moods. He becomes the hero in his own dreams and daydreams. A boy will fantasize being powerful; a girl will fantasize being popular. They become very concerned about "my looks," "my talents," "my disposition," and the thousand and one other facets of the developing personality. But even while the adolescent is living within himself, he has a deep desire to be more extroverted. He becomes lonely when he discovers that being at ease and at home with himself does not necessarily mean he can be at ease with others.

Adolescents as well as children need to be helped with new situations and new people. It is at this time that they can either retreat or force themselves outward. Those who retreat are lonely.

Adolescent loneliness may develop when parents refuse to see the adolescent as a person with his own interests. "My parents never seem to consider whether or not I have any private life or inclinations," one girl reported. "They make their plans and then tell me that I have to stay home and take care of the younger kids while they go out. It makes me feel like a 'nonperson.' It makes me feel lonely."

The adolescent has two alternate cries: "Who am I?" and "I am not a child!" The second is not necessarily in answer to the first, for often it precedes it. No, they are two emotional cries that exist side by side. They are both cries of loneliness. The adolescent hates to be reminded of actions that indicate vestiges of childhood dependency and childish behavior. On the other hand, he hesitates at the threshold of adult responses. Loneliness sets in because he is neither child nor adult and because he does not know whether he can successfully leave his childhood.

Once the individual has coped on a number of occasions with problems and solved or met them in an adult fashion, this loneliness of uncertainty will vanish.

The adolescent may become lonely if he feels that he does not have a grasp of his objectives or cannot make up his mind about things. To him indecision is a sign of childish immaturity and separates him from others. Most adolescents tend to think that their troubles are unique and that they are the only ones so bothered. Adults who work with adolescents or who are parents of adolescents have to make them understand that what they feel is valid but not unusual.

Hostility often masks loneliness. The young person lashes out at others, particularly those close to him, because he feels left out and lonely. He may be too proud to admit that he feels lonely, or perhaps he will not even admit it to himself. In a perverse way he tries to destroy the very relationships he needs and wants.

The lonely adolescent may attempt to mask his true emotional feelings and needs by insisting that he wants to be alone—that he craves solitude. He can appear resentful when urged to take part in activities even while he secretly wishes to become involved. The lonely adolescent, like the lonely adult, may carefully cultivate an "I don't care" attitude. This is deceptive, for he really *does* care but does not know how to manage his life in a way that is more acceptable to his needs.

Excessive drinking, taking drugs, and continuous loud and aggressive behavior are all signs that point to loneliness. The individual feels driven by the emotional pain of loneliness. Unlike adults who can forget some of their problems by immersing themselves in their work, adolescents do not have this same handy excuse. Nor are they experienced enough to have the hope that tomorrow will be better. It is ironic that the adolescent who has the normal expectation of many years to come can rarely be made to understand the concept of "future." Everything in adolescence is concentrated in the present—in today and the person himself. In that respect the adolescent is still very close to childhood. Part of his growing up is acquiring a more mature self-concept and a sense of time and history.

Living and working with adolescents can be rewarding and stimulating—as well as exasperating. They bring a fresh and sensitive outlook to old problems. But they need help, guidance, and love. Sometimes these needs are expressed unconsciously, and you will have to develop an awareness that tells you when a lonely adolescent needs something from you.

9

The Tools of the Fight

Loneliness is a very personal problem. It is centered in the individual. It is a psychological and an emotional condition that affects the total life of the individual. Loneliness alters your personality, determining your outlook on life and your chances of happiness in that life.

You can't share loneliness. It is too personal and individual a problem. You can, however, project loneliness. You can let it run your life, but that won't help you to solve your problem or get over your loneliness.

In the preceding chapters we have suggested a number of ways for you to help yourself fight your personal battle against loneliness. Surely one or more of these solutions can be made to work for you. Do you feel angry with yourself and provoked, perhaps, with us for frankly confronting you with your own shortcomings that contribute to your loneliness? We have bluntly asserted that your own dilatory habits and self-pitying concern have destroyed your will to act in your own behalf and have replaced self-esteem with excuses and complaints. No wonder you are angry—and this is good! There are no better weapons than anger and disgust for combating any enemy. This particular antagonist happens to be an internal culprit. You have probably grown to despise that part of yourself that hinders you from becoming the kind of person you'd like to be—one who is involved with others and with the life going on all around you.

If you feel this anger and disgust with yourself, this is a forward step. It is a step toward making those necessary changes in your life. Picture yourself as going down a dark, unpleasant road—loneliness—and now you come to the decision to turn around, walk back, and find a more pleasant way of going toward your destination. Going back is not easy except for the fact that you know now where you are going and that you are going to improve the way along which you travel.

Yes, it takes courage to turn back—more courage than it takes to plod along in the same path, feeling miserable and complaining—but the eventual rewards are so great that turning back is the only reasonable action to take.

With loneliness you turn back when you decide to

face your problem and to solve it. You do this in terms of your own particular personal background, experiences, and environment.

If in your analysis of your personal dilemma you have realized that you never had a solid family life or a happy, loving childhood and therefore have no inner resources to draw upon, don't think your case is exceptional. Parenthood alone provides no assurance of being able to love. Accept the fact that you were unloved because your parents may have been incapable of loving—not just you, personally, but anyone. Perhaps they were so insecure and neurotic themselves, so crazy or irresponsible, that they had no time or interest to invest in anyone's problems but their own. If this was the case, then that was *their* problem. Don't waste your time waiting, hoping they will find a solution, repent of their failings, and give you the love you long for and have never received. *Your* problem is now, and you are already well on the road to solving it. Recognition of an ailing ego and a cogent diagnosis of its ills are half the cure.

Sarah, for example, was a lonely, unhappy, and bitter middle-aged woman. Although she was attractive and intelligent she had never married, nor did she have any close friends. When asked why she did not have a more adequate social life and why she had not dated, her explanation was that her parents had never permitted her to go out socially. She also complained that she felt socially inferior because her parents, who were themselves lacking in social graces, had not encouraged her to develop the assurance she needed to feel at ease in dating and social affairs.

It was pointed out to Sarah that she was now a grown woman, independent financially as well as emotionally, and that she alone was responsible for her social life. Her willingness to continue to place the blame on her parents for her loneliness showed a lack of maturity. It was only logical to conclude that Sarah was getting more emotional satisfaction out of blaming her parents than out of having a happy life.

In a somewhat similar situation another woman also blamed her parents for her lack of social adjustment and subsequent loneliness, but she finally came to the conclusion that it was foolish of her to ruin her life because of an unsatisfactory relationship with her parents and an unwholesome dependence upon their standards. She then made an effort to break the mold in which her parents had cast her and to remake her personality into one that was more to her liking. She made the effort to get out and meet people. To overcome her social insecurity, she studied books of etiquette until she felt capable of meeting people in all kinds of social and business situations. She got rid of her unhappy, bitter outlook on life, an outlook that had repelled others, and developed a cheerful, outgoing attitude.

To help herself in this transitional period, she busied herself with volunteer work in her local hospital. Working with those in pain and in need helped her to put her own life into perspective and see the positive aspects of her personal situation. Her loneliness problem was solved because she wanted to solve it and took steps to eradicate it from her life. She came to the realization that blaming her parents was too easy a way to get out of living a full life. She also recognized the fact that it wasn't her parents who had cheated her out of that happy life; she was doing it to herself!

If you entertain a healthy hatred for the parents who cheated you of your birthright of parental love, admit it candidly without a feeling of guilt. Don't turn this hatred inward where it creates self-pity and depression.

You can't go back to infancy and retrace your growing up to correct the frailties of personality you now discern. But you can now, today, begin to reshape your life according to the mold of your own desire, avoiding those flaws of personality that have hampered your achieving emotional maturity, independence of spirit, and the ability to go out and get what you want out of life.

This whole process of dispelling loneliness is one of personal activity, and it leaves no room for passive yearning for someone else to come along and make things right for you. What you may have suffered as a child is over and done with. It need not be reexperienced day after day or grieved about or celebrated by way of martyred withdrawal from the world. The past is gone, but "living" is today and now! It is also the time when the future must be planned for.

You would not expect to improve your figure by studying diagrams of body-building exercises. Nor is your lonely life going to be changed one whit by merely reading this book or any other that purports to offer some solutions—some problem-solving exercises—to make you more flexible, to get you out of the rut you have fallen into. You must convince yourself, with the encouragement offered in these pages, that it is possible to change your life and that this wonderful opportunity is something to greet with enthusiasm. This is no task for the physically lazy or the mentally muscle-bound. Besides energy, verve, and imagination, it takes some show of character and determination to repattern your entire life!

Wishing won't make it so despite folktales and popular songs! Wishing is part of it, yes, but action is the second and the bigger part. Wishing is like turning the ignition key in your automobile; it turns the engine on, but you still can't get anywhere until you shift into gear and step on the gas.

To be lonely and wish that you weren't is natural, but to stop at the wishing stage is wrong. You have to go beyond that vague daydream stage into reality. One thing you can do is to get better acquainted with yourself. Knowing more about yourself will help you find the best ways of handling your loneliness problem.

Do you really *know* what kind of person you are?

Have you ever taken the time to sit down and analyze your good qualities or your bad ones? How does one go about knowing himself? Try setting aside some time each day just for meditation. Your self-destroying inner voice will say that you're wasting time that could be applied to more constructive activities, that the whole process is ridiculous. But the art of meditation is no less than four thousand years old, by historic record, as we know from the ancient writings of Oriental philosophers, and the nagging little voice that says it's all silliness and nonsense is unquestionably outclassed!

One of the most famous precepts of all times is the inscription at the Delphic Oracle as recorded by Plutarch—"Know thyself." You can learn to know yourself through meditation. It is a way of getting acquainted with the person you have become, and it also gives you the opportunity of getting to know more about the person you would like to become. The Bible speaks frequently of the value of meditation and uses such phrases as "the meditation of my heart." Other writers, philosophers, and teachers have also spoken highly not only of meditation but of what can be learned through the practice of meditation. As Confucius explained it, "What the superior man seeks is in himself," and it is only in those quiet moments that you can discover what is in yourself. And the value that comes from meditation has best been expressed by St. Francis of Assisi in these words: "Where there is peace and meditation, there is neither anxiety nor doubt." Meditation is a weapon you can use in your private war against loneliness. It has proved down through the ages to be effective in the battle of personality knowledge and development.

But you won't really know until you give it a try, will you? So draw the blinds or dim the lights, and lie down comfortably in some place of utter quiet where you are certain, for a time, at least, to have no interruptions. (Oh, and incidentally, don't forget to turn off the TV!) Now, try to erase from your mind all externals—all distracting images, including grocery lists, news headlines, and any other superficial thought patterns. Try, then, to visualize a clear, cloudless sky, and let us begin to review your life episodically, using the sky as a backdrop.

What is the first picture of yourself that you can see? Can you recapture the image of yourself as a child? Speak aloud any feelings or recollections that come alive with this picture. Are you ashamed to talk aloud to yourself—even when you know there is no one to overhear? Why should you be? What causes this uneasy feeling? It is only your enemy within that is resisting your attempt to explore your mind, telling you that an effort at self-analysis not only is weird and eccentric but stems from an unhealthy kind of curiosity.

Reduce all sensory stimulation to a minimum. You can't direct attention to internal reality if you are distracted by external reality. Experiment as little as fifteen minutes each day. You will be astounded to find how much that you had supposed forgotten is subject to recall from your unconscious. Psychiatrists (including the authors) undergo intensive psychoanalysis as a part of their training. And even though this may last for as long as five years on an average (and frequently longer), with five fifty-minute sessions every week, the process never ends. The recovery of memories and impressions from past experience may be considered in the nature of being retroactive. But your life and its daily experiences go on, creating further reservoirs of thoughts and feelings, of impressions and reactions—also to be examined in moments of meditation. Once the process of analysis begins, the daily practice should be kept up indefinitely. This is what professional psychiatrists do to keep "in form."

Once you have made the practice of meditation a habit, setting aside a few minutes each day to purge your mind of pent-up feelings in a state of quietude and relaxation, you will grow to look forward to the time each day that you reserve for this purpose, just as you look forward to a good hot shower to refresh you physically after a trying day's work.

Many of the thoughts and feelings that emerge may sound foolish to you. Many of the ideas that "surface" in these sessions of meditation seem to have no sound basis in your conscious life. But this is normal: The natural progression of analysis is to let your mind move from feeling to thought, to memory to understanding, and to acceptance. We emphasize the

importance of giving rein to the feelings and emotions, because it should be borne in mind that these
self-analytical exercises are definitely not to be regarded as an intellectual experiment. If you feel like
crying, then cry; or if you feel exultant, laugh or
shout. These are natural emotions straining to be expressed, and you will feel better for "letting go."

Here is a typical example of the way the emotion
of fear, let us say, is explored and uncovered. A person lies down, clears his mind, and thinks of himself
as a frightened child. His thoughts are saying, "I am
scared . . . of what? . . . scared of monsters . . . what
monsters? . . . the one hiding in the closet . . . which
closet? . . . the one in my little room . . . I'm five, and
nobody loves me . . . they all seem like monsters . . .
my father . . . he frightens me with his hard, cold
face, his big hand . . . then all the other people seem
like him . . . better to run and hide from everyone
because they might scare me the way he does."

This person sought loneliness because of a hang-
over of childhood fears. He recognized that he was
transferring his fear of an abusive father onto everyone in his adult life. This was unfair to others as well
as to himself. He might never have come to this realization but could have lived out his life withdrawn
from the warmth of close human relationships had he
not overcome his fears and emotional bias by means
of self-analysis through meditation. What a difference
once he began to experience his fellowmen as indi-

viduals rather than as prototypes of a frightening, unloving father figure.

Self-discovery through quiet meditation is the first
step in becoming involved with others. Through its
disciplines you are able to get close to your own inner
thoughts and feelings, and with this understanding of
self you are then able to interact with others.

There is nothing unique about the inner life you
discover. Everyone has such an "other self" hidden
away from the self he thinks he is and from the outer
self that other people recognize. All of us are many
persons. One should not become alarmed when, during the course of these meditative processes, angry,
even violent, feelings come to the surface. It is good
that they do. These are only daydreams, fitful fantasies and emotions, not actual deeds. If you feel re-
vengeful toward persons who hurt you as a child, or
later as an adult, indulge in the fantasy of avenging
yourself upon them. In this way you can discharge
these feelings of hatred and vengeance, clearing your
mind and heart for the acceptance of other people.

One should not allow past slights and injuries to
dwell in one's mind. They are not only destructive of
personal happiness but also damaging to physical
health. It's like throwing off a heavy pack from your
back; once you have learned to discipline your mental
processes so that you can relive the injustices of your
past, take your revenge, and then bury it once and
for all time.

With the clearing away of all this emotional rubbish and the cleansing of your mind of bitter bygone injuries, whether real or imagined, the next step is to extend yourself to some other person. Take advantage of opportunities for involvement that you have scorned or ignored in the past. You will now find yourself noticing the needs of others, so like your own. You will find you are able to reap friendship and love because of your understanding response to the desperation of others—a perceptivity that would not have been possible while all your attention and sympathies were centered on your own travails.

A sense of humor is an invaluable tool for extricating yourself from your shell of solitude. There is nothing like laughter for gaining some perspective about yourself. Even the things you worry about can be funny if you have acquired the perspective to see them in that light.

A realistic outlook concerning the span of human life, or for that matter, of human life upon the universe, is a useful tool for eradicating so many of the ills that beset the human race. You don't have to read a history book—think of your own family history. Consider how many of your own family or of your contemporaries have died within your lifetime. Think of the many famous public figures whose obituaries you read day after day. Famous or unknown, rich or poor, ugly or beautiful—all these have made their little splash and moved on. The concept of time and the universe is unfathomable unless one has the perspective to relate his own self to such cosmic magnitudes. This is the field of the Einsteins, of which all historic time can name but few. But it is possible for each of us to develop the insight that shows the absurdity of dallying away that precious, brief interlude between birth and death that we are here upon this earth. With this much perspective we have the tools for quieting that stupid inner voice that counsels us to withdraw from the world and life's many opportunities for meaningful involvements. Use these tools with the knowledge that you have only one chance at life. Work with diligence to know yourself and your own feelings. Extend your range outward by being aware of what lies inward. If you genuinely want to conquer loneliness, you will!

Index

174

Escaping (*cont.*)
solving problems in place
of, 81–104
Ethnic groups, loneliness and,
6–7
Extroversion, adolescent loneliness and, 158

Failure, loneliness and fear
of
adolescent, 145–146
childhood, 135–136, 140
Family, loneliness and, 8 ff.,
68–73, 163–166, 170–171,
172
adolescents and, 142–160
breakdown of unit and sub-
stitutes for, 121–124
changes and situational, 40,
41 ff., 153–154
children and, 8 ff., 26 ff., 69–
73, 126–140
See also Children, loneliness and
and "togetherness," 6–7
See also Marriage, loneliness and; Parent-child
relationship
Fantasies, *see* Daydreaming
Fathers, *see* Family, loneliness and; Parent-child
relationship
Fatigue, loneliness and, 38, 39,
62, 65–66, 75, 96–97, 98
urban living and, 106–107,
109
See also Sleeplessness,
loneliness and
Fear, 66, 103–104
adolescent loneliness and,
145 ff.
childhood loneliness and,
135–140

meditation and overcoming,
170–171
unconscious, 75–80
See also Unconscious, the,
emotional problems
and loneliness and
See also Anxiety; Inse-
curity, emotional
Food, loneliness and, 3, 4, 123,
128
dieting and, 33–34
digestion and, 38, 65, 83–84
oral dependency and childhood and, 128
overeating, 3, 4, 33–34, 39,
67, 88–89, 96, 128
Francis of Assisi, St., 167–168
Friendship, 23–24, 26–37, 45,
46, 47, 66, 72, 76–80, 83–
84, 110–111, 113, 119, 172
computer-arranged, 90–95
situational loneliness and,
42 ff.
See also Group involve-
ment, overcoming lone-
liness in; Love, over-
coming loneliness and;
Personal involvement;
Personal relationships
Future, the, loneliness and
concept of, 160
See also Time, overcoming
loneliness and concept
of

Generation gap, loneliness in
adolescence and, 149–
153
Gettysburg Address, 14
Goethe, Johann von, 141
Graham, Billy, 5
Grandparents, adoptive, 95–
96

Grief, 165
  death and loneliness and,
    56–61
  See also Depression, loneliness and; Despair
Group culture, 5–10, 21–22
  aloneness and emphasis on,
    5–10, 21–22
  communes and, 7–8
Group involvement, overcoming loneliness in, 23–24,
    44–47, 61
  See also Club membership,
    overcoming loneliness
    and; Friendship; Personal involvement; Volunteer or service work,
    overcoming loneliness
    and
Guilt feelings, 165

Happiness, 18, 63
  See also Unhappiness, and
    loneliness
Headaches, loneliness as
  cause of, 63, 65–66, 68
Health, loneliness and, 63–64,
    65–66, 89–90, 171
  urban living and, 106–107,
    110, 113
  See also Physical problems
    and symptoms, loneliness and
Hearing ability, noise in
  urban areas and, 112–113
Hippie communes, 7–8
  See also Communes
Hobbies, 55–56, 102, 143–144
  See also Interests, personal;
    Recreation
Holidays, 121
  change and, 121

loneliness and suicide and,
  2
  See also Recreation
Hospital volunteer work, 164–165
Hostility
  adolescents and, 159
  situational loneliness and,
    39, 66
  See also Aggressive impulses, adolescent loneliness and; Anger; Violence
Humor, loneliness and sense
  of, 172
Hypochondria, 89–90

Illness, loneliness and, *see*
  Emotional problems,
  loneliness and; Physical
  problems and symptoms, loneliness and;
  Psychosomatic illnesses
Imaginative faculty, solitude
  and development of,
    8–9
  See also Creativity
Immaturity, *see* Emotional
  problems, loneliness
  and
Independence, *see* Dependency
Indigestion, loneliness and,
  38, 65, 83–84
Individualism, group action
  and, 6, 8
Infants, 26–27
  See also Children, loneliness and
Inner self, *see* Unconscious,
  the, emotional problems
  and loneliness and

childhood loneliness and, 138–139

family breakdown and, 122–124

love and sharing and, 25–37

overcoming loneliness and, 23 ff., 44–47, 76–80, 83 ff., 122–124, 163–166, 171, 172

social, 96, 98–99

solving problems of, 23 ff., 64–80, 83–104

urban living and, 107–108, 110–111, 113, 119

See also Family, loneliness and; Friendship; Parent-child relationship; Personal involvement

Personality

adolescent loneliness and, 142–160 *passim*

dependency and, 8–16

See also Dependency

ego and ego impingements and, 107 ff.

emotional problems and, *see* Emotional problems, loneliness and

loneliness as a way of life and, 62–80

overcoming loneliness and, 142–160 *passim*

personal relationships and, 28–37

See also Personal relationships

self-exploration and awareness and, 28–37 *passim*

See also Self-analysis

situational loneliness and changes in, 39–69 *passim*

Photography, as a hobby, 55, 143–144

Physical appearance, *see* Personal appearance

Physical problems and symptoms, loneliness and, 4, 38–39, 63–64, 65–66, 68, 83, 84, 89–90, 171

children and, 127–128

disabilities and, 4, 97–98

psychosomatic illnesses and, 4, 64, 65–66

urban living and, 106–107, 110, 113

Pollution, urban living and loneliness and, 107, 111, 112–113, 150

Popularity, adolescent loneliness and importance of, 155–156, 157

Population density, *see* Overcrowding

Pressures

suicide and, 3

See also Suicide, loneliness and

urban living and, 105 ff.

See also Stress situations; Tensions

Privacy, 16

See also Aloneness; Solitude

Professional organizations, "togetherness" and, 7

Psychology Today, 59

Psychosomatic illnesses, 4, 64, 65–66

Puberty, 142

See also Adolescents, loneliness and

Reading and discussion groups, overcoming loneliness and, 103, 123

Rebelliousness, adolescent
loneliness and, 146–149
See also Misbehavior
Recreation, 121, 134–135
See also Hobbies; Interests,
personal
Rejection, loneliness and, 31,
35–36
in childhood, 126 ff., 131–134
fear of, 35–36
Responsibility, 164
acceptance of, 24
love and, 27
Retirement, loneliness and
aging and, 40, 52–56
preparation for, 54–56
Robbins, Dr. Edwin S., 3–4
Robbins, Dr. William, 3–4
Role-playing, adolescent loneliness and, 154–155

St. Petersburg (Fla.), retirement community in, 54
Salinger, J. D., 141
Security, emotional, *see* Insecurity, emotional
Self-analysis, 14, 19–20, 28–
29, 30–37, 70–71, 99–101,
102–104, 107, 109, 142–
143, 166–173
Self-centeredness, 29, 31, 35–
37, 63, 71, 73, 102
Self-concept, *see* Self-image
Self-confidence, overcoming
loneliness and, 11, 12–13,
26, 32, 33–35, 41, 68–69,
76, 79–80, 87, 103 ff., 124,
140, 162, 163 ff.
Self-consciousness, 33–34, 75–
80, 103–104, 163 ff.
Self-critical attitudes and
feelings, 32–33, 41, 79–80

See also Criticalness, and
personal relationships
Self-image, 29–37, 39, 146–151,
158–159, 160, 163 ff.
Self-improvement, overcoming loneliness and, 33–
34, 101–104
Self-pity, loneliness and, 2, 27,
29, 63, 66, 70, 162, 165
Self-reliance, loneliness and,
11 ff.
See also Dependency
Self-reproach, *see* Self-critical
attitudes and feelings
Sensitivity
ego impingements and, 107
overcoming loneliness and
development of, 124
Sermon on the Mount, 13–
14
Service, *see* Volunteer or
service work, overcom-
ing loneliness and
Seventeen (Tarkington), 141
Sexual drives, adolescent
loneliness and, 151–152
Sharing, overcoming loneliness and, 16, 25–37, 46–
47, 51, 52, 71, 123–124
children and, 134–135
love and, 25–37
See also Love, overcom-
ing loneliness and
urban living and, 108
volunteer or service work
and, 51, 52, 79, 94–96,
164–165
See also Friendship; Personal involvement
Siblings, childhood loneliness
and, 131–132, 136–138
adolescent loneliness and,
156